Pioneer American Railroads:

THE MOHAWK AND HUDSON
&
THE SARATOGA and SCHENECTADY

By F. Daniel Larkin
John B. Jervis: An American Engineering Pioneer
1990

By F. Daniel Larkin, et al.
New York Yesterday and Today
1985

Cover:
Watercolor drawing of the locomotive Experiment by John B. Jervis.
Courtesy of the Jervis Collection

Pioneer American Railroads:

THE MOHAWK AND HUDSON
&
THE SARATOGA AND SCHENECTADY

by F. Daniel Larkin

PURPLE MOUNTAIN PRESS

Fleischmanns, New York

Pioneer American Railroads:
The Mohawk and Hudson & The Saratoga and Schenectady

FIRST EDITION
1995

Published by
PURPLE MOUNTAIN PRESS, LTD.
Main Street, P.O. Box E3
Fleischmanns, New York 12430-0378
914-254-4062
914-254-4476 (fax)

Library of Congress Cataloging-in-Publication Data

Larkin, F. Daniel, 1938-
    Pioneer American railroads : The Mohawk and Hudson & the Saratoga
and Schenectady / by F. Daniel Larkin. -- 1st ed.
        p.   cm.
    Includes bibliographical references (p.   -   ) and index.
    ISBN 0-935796-71-1 (alk. paper)
    1. Mohawk and Hudson Rail Road Company.   2. Saratoga and
Schenectady Rail Road.   3. Railroads--New York (State)   I. Title.
TF25.M63L37   1995   95-41702
385'.09747- -dc20   CIP

Manufactured in the United States of America.
Printed on acid-free paper.

To Kathy and Susan who never knew the great days of railroading.

ACKNOWLEDGMENTS

Among those who have graciously assisted me in preparing this book are
the staffs of the Jervis Library in Rome, New York; the New York State Library in Albany;
the Library of the Albany Institute of History and Art; and the Library of Congress, Washington, D.C.

Please note:
Some of the engineering drawings in this book are
reproduced from lightly drawn, faded originals. The author
and the publisher believe they should be included because of their
historic significance even though contrasts are poor.

Table of Contents

This unknown locomotive of English design may have been one of those ordered for the Mohawk and Hudson or for the Delaware and Hudson's gravity railroad. Since it appears to be a Stephenson Planet-class design, however, this would preclude the Delaware and Hudson order of 1829. The Planet was introduced in 1830.

Courtesy of the Jervis Collection

Introduction

PICTURE the United States at the end of the first quarter of the nineteenth century. It was a sprawling nation that stretched from the Atlantic Ocean to the Rockies. Yet most of its population of more than ten million lived east of the Mississippi River. Only two of its twenty-four states—Missouri and Louisiana—were west of that great waterway. The United States was still a young country, and in 1826 celebrated the fiftieth anniversary of its Declaration of Independence. The principal author of that hallowed document, Thomas Jefferson, died on the very day of the celebration, July 4. John Adams, Jefferson's predecessor in the presidential office and old political rival, expired on the same day. Adams lived long enough, however, to see his son John Quincy become president. The younger Adams took office in 1825.

By 1826, the "Founding Fathers" were passing from the nation that they helped create. A new generation of politicians, perhaps less imbued with the nobler ideals of governance, was emerging to take the place of the Revolutionary War generation. Many among the new politicians were New Yorkers, who supplanted Virginians as the nation's political leaders. Symbolically, Virginia, the state that produced several of the nation's leading political architects of the passing age, relinquished its population predominance as well. In 1820, New York had surpassed Virginia as the country's most populous state.

After the Revolutionary War, New York's population grew rapidly as waves of newcomers, mainly from New England, sought the relatively unsettled land west of the Hudson River. This "Yankee Invasion" commenced at the end of the Revolution and continued into the 1830s. But, just as New England's burgeoning hordes moved westward in search of agricultural "elbow room," commerce and industry began to challenge farming as a leading source of income in the northeastern and mid-Atlantic regions. As this phenomenon gained momentum, eastern merchants and manufacturers looked to the hinterlands as a source for agricultural produce and other raw materials. In return, the ever-advancing westward expansion engendered a seemingly insatiable appetite for the manufactured goods coming from the East. Theoretically, one section could have complemented the other economically. But a major obstacle stood in the way of this exchange: lack of adequate and inexpensive transportation.

Prior to the 1820s, the only practical way to transfer bulk items, such as the produce of the west, was via water. Land transportation, where it existed, was very costly and slow. For centuries, rivers had provided the best method of moving people and goods to the seaboard. This system was tolerated as long as the movement was mainly east of the Appalachian Mountains. Once large-scale settlement began to shift west of that mountain barrier, streams were less valuable for transportation purposes.

It was not that the trans-Appalachian west lacked rivers. The problem was that the natural waterways ran in the wrong direction: Many of the streams west of the mountains eventually found their way into the Ohio River which, in turn, flowed south-westerly into the Mississippi, whose outlet was the Gulf of Mexico. Such an arrangement did not serve well the direct, east-west trade.

Nevertheless, in the first quarter of the nineteenth century, Americans accepted the topographic challenge and, with New Yorkers taking the lead, began to dig their way west. New York capitalized on its unique, natural water-level route through the mountains and by 1825 opened the 350-mile-long Erie Canal from Albany on the Hudson River to Buffalo on Lake Erie. This had the effect of shortening the way west and tapping the bounty of the interior. New York's great canal project was immensely successful, to be sure. But even with the completion of the new artificial waterway, it still took nearly four days to reach Buffalo from New York City, almost two weeks overland to the Mississippi, and more than five weeks to the western end of Lake Superior.

The Erie Canal was so successful it set off a digging frenzy throughout the northern and western sections of the country in an attempt to match New

York's accomplishment and envisioned prosperity. Canals seemed to be the transportation promise of the future, and money poured into these ditches in amazing amounts.

This, curiously, is where the story of New York's first railroad had its start. The building of another canal during the post-Erie Canal boom led to the construction not only of an early railroad but of the first railroad in the nation designed specifically to use steam locomotives. The tale of the Empire State's first "iron road" becomes even more complex, since the precedent and practice for its pioneer line took place not in New York—the state that took the initiative to finance and build that transportation marvel, the "Great Western Canal," as the Erie often was called—but in the hills of northeastern Pennsylvania. It was there that a railway constructed under the aegis of the Delaware and Hudson Canal Company commenced the series of events that resulted in railroad building in New York.

Several accounts exist of the Mohawk and Hudson, New York's first railroad. When the road opened for business, S. DeWitt Bloodgood published a description in the *American Journal of Science and Arts* (January 1832). In 1876, a half century after the railroad was chartered, Joel Munsell's "The Mohawk and Hudson Railroad" appeared in the *Transactions of the Albany Institute*. Another fifty years passed before Frank Walker Stevens offered an excellent history of New York's initial line in the first chapter of his 1926 landmark, *The Beginnings of the New York Central Railroad*. Unfortunately, the book contains few citations to indicate the sources used by the author. The Mohawk and Hudson Railroad was again discussed in the opening chapter of Edward Hungerford's *Men and Iron: The History of the New York Central*, printed in 1938. *Men and Iron* reiterated much of what appeared in the Stevens book because, apparently, Hungerford took most of his material from Stevens. Five years after the publication of *Men and Iron*, the Mohawk and Hudson was again recognized in T. V. Flannery's short historical account presented to the Albany County Historical Associa-

tion. Later, in 1947, the early railroad's history was chronicled by Alvin F. Harlow in *The Road of the Century: The Story of the New York Central*. Harlow borrowed freely from earlier historians for his popularized version.

Then, after a hiatus of a quarter of a century, more information on the building of New York's first railroad appeared when civil engineer Neal FitzSimons edited John B. Jervis's "autobiography," which was published as *The Reminiscences of John B. Jervis: Engineer of the Old Croton*. Next came the brief but informative history by Fred B. Abele, *The Mohawk and Hudson Railroad Co., 1826-1853*, printed in 1981. Also available is an unpublished master's thesis completed by John DeMis a few years after Abele's work. DeMis's paper is a useful contribution to the study of New York's first railroad since its focus is on the location of the original route of the Mohawk and Hudson.

The purpose of the history presented here is to examine the precedents of New York's first railroad and to reexamine the story of this pioneer railway. The publication in 1990 of *John B. Jervis: An American Engineering Pioneer*, the biography of the engineer who successfully completed the Mohawk and Hudson, brought additional information about the railroad's construction to light. As Jervis also built the second railroad in New York—the Saratoga and Schenectady, which was constructed as an adjunct to the Mohawk and Hudson—development of this line also will be discussed.

The focus of this work is upon early railroad technology. The extent to which ideas for technological modernization were imported from abroad will be examined, as well as innovative proposals of Americans who advocated and implemented changes to the transportation system of the United States. In this sense, this also is a brief history of the United States in general—and New York State, in particular—during the period 1825 through 1853, with emphasis upon the primary development of a machine that dominated the American transportation scene between the middle of the nineteenth and middle of the twentieth centuries.

I: The Land of Railroads

HORATIO ALLEN'S thoughts must have raced ahead of the bow wave as his ship plowed through the murky North Atlantic on its voyage to England. He probably wondered what sights he would behold in that nation where steam-powered locomotives were being built and run with an ever increasing regularity. Allen left an America in late 1827 where there were no locomotives, and scarcely even animal-powered railroads. He was headed to the country that opened "the world's first public railway" in 1825.[1] The Stockton and Darlington Railroad was an immediate success. It carried not only thousands of passengers but also hundreds of thousands of tons of coal,[2] the latter traffic undoubtedly of particular interest to the young traveler from the United States.

The twenty-six-year-old Allen's mission to the "land of railroads . . . in the atmosphere of coal smoke"[3] was to purchase four locomotives for the relatively new Delaware and Hudson Canal Company. If this seemed a strange assignment for a representative of a canal company, it could be easily explained. The chief purpose of the as yet unfinished Delaware and Hudson Canal was to carry coal from the mines in northeastern Pennsylvania to tidewater for distribution. To the Delaware and Hudson Company, tidewater was the Hudson River at Kingston, New York, approximately ninety miles north of New York City. Due to the hilly terrain in the area of the mines, the first sixteen miles of the coal route was to be a railroad. The project's two principal engineers, Benjamin Wright and John Jervis, decided that in addition to horse power, the railroad would use locomotives and even stationary steam engines to pull coal-laden cars to the head of the canal. This was a bold decision, since there were no steam locomotives in operation anywhere on the entire continent.

Yet the use of new technology was in keeping with the mining of coal as the new fuel to warm American buildings and eventually to power America's rapidly spreading industrialization. Coal was more dependable than water power, and more efficient at heat production than wood—a property that was also exploited by the designers and builders of steamships. Thus, by the second half of the nineteenth century, coal became the fuel of choice to drive America's industrial machinery and heat its buildings. But in the second quarter of the nineteenth century, Americans were only optimistically envisioning coal's beneficial place in national expansion and modernization. At that time, and throughout the remainder of the century, little attention was paid to the its drawbacks.

Among those who envisioned a prosperous future for coal were Maurice and William Wurts, Philadelphia merchants who acquired tracts of land for recreational use in the sparsely settled northeast portion of Pennsylvania. Hunting trips to their acreage acquainted them with the abundant anthracite out-

Horatio Allen.

croppings of the region. By 1822, they commenced serious mining in the vicinity of a community that became known as Carbondale. After failed attempts to sell their coal in Philadelphia due to competition from sources closer to that city, the Wurts brothers began to look to the New York market. But an inexpensive way to ship their bulk commodity to the expanding metropolis at the mouth of the Hudson River was needed.[4] At that time, a canal was the obvious answer. To accomplish their goal, the Wurts brothers first secured the services of one of the most renowned engineers in the nation to survey a route for the waterway. Then they carried samples of their product to New York City to sell their idea to the men with the money.

In the spring of 1823, the Wurts brothers hired Benjamin Wright to lay out the best route from the high country of northeastern Pennsylvania to the Hudson. Born in Connecticut in 1770, Wright migrated to central New York at age twenty and began his civil engineering education as a land surveyor. Within a decade of his arrival he was employed by a company that built several very short canals in an

Benjamin Wright, 1770-1842.
The Father of American Civil Engineering.

From: *A Biographical Dictionary of American Civil Engineers*, New York: American Society of Civil Engineers, 1972. Reproduced by permission of the publisher.

effort to improve the natural waterway system between the Hudson River and Lake Ontario. When construction began on the Erie Canal in 1817, Wright was named a principal engineer and soon became chief of the entire project. From that time, his career commenced a meteoric rise that insured his preeminence among American civil engineers and brought him constant project commissions until his death in 1842.

When the Wurts brothers succeeded in luring Wright to the Delaware and Hudson venture, he was still employed on the unfinished Erie Canal, was a member of the engineering board of the Chesapeake and Delaware Canal, and was consulting engineer on the James River Canal in Virginia. Although he surveyed at least two routes for the Wurts brothers' canal and directed other planning and operations, Wright spent relatively little time on the project, particularly after 1825. On the other hand, due to his nearly unfailing ability to choose assistants wisely, he did not have to give much attention to the Delaware and Hudson construction: In 1825, Wright's choice of an engineer to serve as his principal assistant was John B. Jervis.

Early in 1825, with the renowned Wright's feasibility report in hand, Maurice and William Wurts staged a demonstration in New York City designed to raise the capital to build the canal. On January 7, the two men heated a meeting room at the Tontine Coffee House on Wall Street with Pennsylvania coal to convince the New York capitalists of the value of their proposed venture. The sales pitch worked, and stock in the new Delaware and Hudson Canal Company was quickly subscribed. Two months later, again at the Tontine Coffee House, an organizational meeting was held and directors were elected. Among the board members was Lynde Catlin, who became one of the initial directors of the Mohawk and Hudson Railroad Company a year later. Philip Hone, mayor of New York City, was named president of the new company. The canal dream of the Wurts brothers—along with it, a railroad—was about to become a reality.[5]

On March 12, 1825, the day after Philip Hone became company president, Benjamin Wright selected John Jervis as his number-two man in the canal company's engineering department. The thirty-year-old Jervis, a New Yorker by birth, learned his trade on the Erie project. Since the great waterway was nearing completion, Jervis decided to accept Wright's invitation to come to New York City. Although Wright headed the Delaware and Hudson

Canal construction until 1827, it was Jervis who actually organized the engineering department and directed the construction. In this role, Jervis also drew up the final plans for the company's railway.[6] The future builder of the Mohawk and Hudson Railroad was acquiring his iron road education.

The initial planning for the railroad, which would stretch from the mines at Carbondale to the head of canal at Honesdale, was done by Benjamin Wright. He reported to the company directors in 1825 and again in 1826 on the proposed railway across the Moosic Mountains. Evidence strongly suggests that Wright relied considerably on Jervis's surveys and advice. But the experienced Wright tended to be cautious in his recommendations to the company, and he counseled that "we have no experience in this country of railways."[7] Wright advised constructing a wagon road adjacent to the track at least part of the distance between Carbondale and Honesdale as a backup should the railroad fail. Clearly though, he was not opposed to railroad construction; his report included considerable technical data to help make it possible.[8]

When Jervis succeeded Wright as chief engineer early in 1827, his first important assignment was to conduct another survey for the railroad. By October 22, he made a long, detailed report to the company directors. "Report of the Projected Carbondale Railroad" relied considerably on his study of English experience. In this country, only the short Quincy Railroad, which Jervis observed in Boston, and the unfinished Mauch Chunk gravity railroad in Pennsylvania could have served as models. But neither railroad provided for the use of locomotives, as Jervis's plan did. Much of the background that Jervis brought to the Mohawk and Hudson Railroad was gained from his research preparatory to building the Carbondale gravity line.

Jervis's completed report, which was sent to Benjamin Wright for his comments and also was reviewed by James Renwick, a professor at Columbia University and a future director of the Mohawk and Hudson Company, considered railway design, rail structure and material, as well as motive power and traction. For example, ever mindful of economy, Jervis familiarized himself with the works of English engineers on single-rail railroads. He agreed with those who felt that there was no substantial reduction of friction, nor was there a savings in construction costs. (Although only one rail was needed, the deeper and wider excavation necessary on both sides of the track to provide for the carriages that straddled the

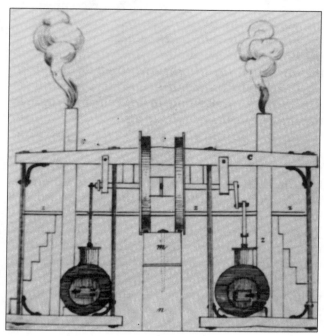

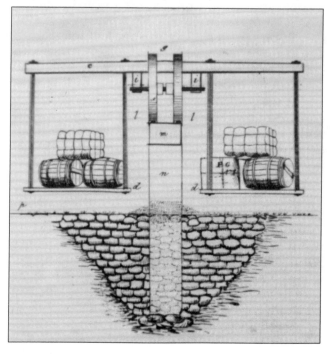

The single-rail railway. *Top:* horse powered. *Middle:* steam powered. *Bottom:* construction detail.
Author's collection

15

track would more than overcome the savings.) Jervis opted for two rails. When it came to a decision on whether to use cast or rolled iron for the plates that would cap the rails, he could see little difference but was "inclined to give preference to rolled iron."[9]

On the subject of power, Jervis recommended the use of thirty-five horsepower stationary steam engines to pull the three-ton loaded cars up the railroad's five inclined planes. Gravity would move the cars down the inclines, the speed of the loaded cars checked by having them pull empty cars up the parallel track on the same plane. (The tow rope for the empty cars passed around a horizontal pulley at the top of the incline.) For the level or nearly level sections of the line less than a mile long, Jervis recommended the use of horse power. On the three remaining levels he decided in favor of locomotives. Before arriving at this decision, he consulted the work of engineers Nicholas Wood and Thomas Tredgold, whose tests in England dealt with the effects of coal dust on wheel-to-rail adhesion. To their data Jervis added relative precipitation characteristics for England and Pennsylvania and concluded that, unlike the weather in England, the hard rains of the American Northeast would wash away coal dust in a manner not done in England. After calculating friction, speed, and load, Jervis estimated the ideal weight for the seven engines that would be needed at six and one-quarter to six and one-half tons each.[10] The locomotive weight specifications were included in the directions he gave to Horatio Allen before the latter left for England.

At first, Allen was overcome with English progress in railroads. He sent Jervis detailed descriptions of the Liverpool and Manchester Railroad, then under construction, and of the operation of the Stockton and Darlington line, England's first passenger railroad. Allen's sightseeing activities may have whetted Jervis's constant thirst for knowledge, but the chief engineer of the Delaware and Hudson had company operations foremost in mind. Jervis wrote to his young agent that he was anxious to receive Allen's "letter on the question of locomotive engines."[11] Although Allen had arranged a meeting with Robert Stephenson, "the expert of the kingdom on steam engines," relatively soon after his arrival, he seemed unable to come to terms for the locomotive purchases. The growing impatience of his boss spurred Allen to action. Finally, by July 1828, he signed contracts with Foster, Rastrick and Company of Stourbridge for three locomotives, and arranged

for Robert Stephenson and Company to build a fourth engine.

Between mid-January and mid-September of 1829, the Foster, Rastrick engines, the Stourbridge Lion, Delaware, and Hudson, arrived in New York City, as did the Stephenson locomotive America. Both the Stourbridge Lion and America were placed on blocks, tested successfully, and put on public display for six weeks.[12] Although records show transportation was arranged for both machines via Hudson River ship and canal boat to the head of the canal at Honesdale, only the Stourbridge Lion arrived at its destination. The America mysteriously disappeared in transit, and the other Foster, Rastrick locomotives apparently never left New York City.[13]

The tracks of early American railroads, like those of the sixteen-mile Delaware and Hudson, were built using substantial, square wood beams, usually oak or white pine, as the rails. The train wheels actually rode upon an iron "cap" or strip approximately two inches wide and roughly one-half inch thick, fastened to the top of the wood rails with iron spikes. The wood rails rested on square granite blocks, each set several inches into the earth. The rails were not tied together by the familiar wooden sleepers or cross-ties until the early 1830s. Hence, one rail often was higher or lower than the other, depending on ground and weather conditions. Widely spaced iron "ties" connected the rails in an attempt to keep them more or less parallel. It was the timber-and-iron capped construction of the rails coupled with a locomotive that exceeded specifications that doomed what would have been the first successful utilization of a locomotive on an American railroad.

Two years before the arrival of the Stourbridge Lion, Jervis calculated that an engine weight not to exceed six and one-half tons would be the most the rails could bear. He planned for a six-wheeled locomotive, which also would increase the tractive force (or pulling power). By 1828, Jervis had changed his mind about six wheels, since he thought they would not hold to the track of a curved railway when mounted on a single frame. He also had second thoughts about the engine weight, and advised Allen that the four-wheeled locomotive should not weigh more than five and a half tons. Unfortunately, Allen neglected to observe the advice from his chief—the Stourbridge Lion weighed eight tons including a ton of fuel and boiler water. The engine exceeded the maximum load capacity of the track by 50 percent.[14]

On August 8, 1829, Horatio Allen climbed aboard the engineer's platform and the Lion was run

Replica of Stourbridge Lion on modern railroad flat car.
Author's collection

out for trials. The event took place under the watchful eye of chief engineer Jervis, who noted that during the test, "one of the capts [iron caps on the wooden rail] began to fail."[15] Still, Jervis felt the locomotive was a good machine and that the rails could be strengthened in order to bear the increased weight. But this was not to be; another run of the Lion on September 9 proved Jervis's original calculations regarding weight. The locomotive impressed the iron cap into the wood rail, and there was nothing for the wheel flanges (inside edges) to butt against in transit. The Stourbridge Lion could not be used on the railroad of the Delaware and Hudson Company—it simply would not be able to stay on the track.[16]

Those who saw the Stourbridge Lion in New York City and who witnessed its trials in Pennsylvania must have thought it an incredible and formidable machine. With its smokestack standing more than twelve feet above its ten-foot long, four-foot diameter boiler of one-half-inch-thick iron plate, the sturdy locomotive must have appeared a model of England's state-of-the-art technology. Added to this bulk were the two massive eight-and-one-half-inch diameter cylinders, each having a thirty-six-inch stroke. They were vertically mounted at each side of the rear of the boiler. The cylinders transferred power to the four forty-eight-inch diameter drive wheels by walking beams connected by vertical rods to the rear wheels. Horizontal rods from the rear

17

All that remains of the original Stourbridge Lion. *Above, left:* Boiler, right cylinder, left walking beam, bottom portion of smokestack. *Above, right:* Detail of vertically mounted cylinder. *Below:* Details of boiler construction.
Smithsonian Institution Museum of American History

drive wheels provided power to the forward pair of wheels. The wheel spokes were wood and the hubs cast iron.[17]

Although the Lion must have seemed the epitome of modern locomotive technology to Americans, it actually was a dated, single-flue boiler colliery machine. The British had been building them for at least fifteen years, and in 1829, they were about to be rendered obsolete.[18] Only one aspect of the Lion could be considered a pioneer feature—the placement of balance weights, or counterweights, on the rear driving wheels. The counterweights were placed on the drive wheels opposite the fastening point of the connecting rods. The purpose of the weights was to assist in the initial rotation of the wheels when the locomotive was put in motion. This was "the earliest known use of counterweights for locomotives," and their use soon became a standard design feature. Even if the Delaware and Hudson Company had known of this pioneering feature, it would have been small

consolation for a company that had spent nearly $3,000 on an engine that could not be used for its intended purpose.[19]

Jervis, undaunted by the failure, continued to believe in the future of locomotives. So did Allen, his protégé, who foresaw locomotive evolution early in 1828 when he predicted that "the present locomotive engine is an imperfect machine compared with what it will be 10 or 12 years hence."[20] Little did both men know that events in England would soon prove their faith in the future of steam locomotives when, in the words of one railroad historian, "the modern world was conceived."[21]

That momentous event took place at Rainhill in England on October 8, 1829, two months to the day after the first running of the Stourbridge Lion. The "Rainhill Trials" were held to determine the kind of locomotives that would be used on the Liverpool and Manchester Railroad, then under construction. The victory at Rainhill went to the Rocket, a small but reliable machine built by Robert Stephenson.[22]

Eleven months later, the Liverpool and Manchester line officially opened amid fanfare that would have been hilarious had it not been marred by the tragic loss of life. What undoubtedly was overlooked in the railroad's introductory hoopla was the fact that the Rocket was itself about to be relegated to museum status by another Stephenson design, manifested in a new engine named Northumbrian.[23]

The novel design of the Rocket that contributed to its success at Rainhill included both a multi-tubular boiler and a blast pipe. The advantage of a boiler containing many small tubes over the older single-flue boilers was the greater surface area of the tubes. The hot gases moving through the tubes could more efficiently heat the water, which made the boiler more efficient at raising steam. The blast pipe enabled the discharge of a jet of steam through the smokestack. This created a partial vacuum; the air that came in to fill the vacuum entered through the fire grate at the opposite end of the boiler. Thus, the amount of heat produced by the blast of air drawn through the fire was dependent upon the amount of steam discharged through the smokestack.[24]

The newer Northumbrian, which led the procession at the opening of the Liverpool and Manchester, contained the heating advances used in the Rocket. But, the Northumbrian also had a smokebox at the front of the locomotive in which the ashes from the firebox could accumulate and be removed. Also, its boiler was integral with the water jacket surrounding the firebox. The design changes in this 1830 locomotive became standard for nearly all steam locomotives built subsequently. In addition to the internal changes on the Northumbrian, the positioning of its cylinders became a model for future cylinder configuration—they were lowered to a nearly horizontal position.[25] By comparison, the cylinders of the Stourbridge Lion were arranged vertically; those of the Rocket were at a thirty-five degree angle. All of these important changes took place before New York's first line opened for business. But their impact was felt upon New York's first railroad enterprise, whose beginnings occurred the same year as the opening of the Stockton and Darlington in England. Ultimately, the lessons learned by both Jervis and Allen from the failure of the gravity line's locomotive experiment in Pennsylvania were turned into future successes elsewhere.

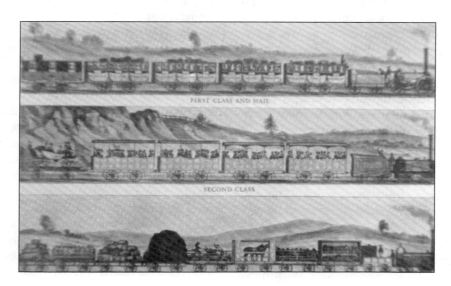

Locomotives and carriages of the Liverpool and Manchester Railway.
Author's collection

II: The Beginnings

A momentous celebration commenced on October 26, 1825, to mark the official opening of New York's impressive Erie Canal. The forty-foot-wide, four-foot-deep artificial waterway joined the Hudson River, and therefore the Atlantic Ocean, with the Great Lakes. A flotilla carrying Governor DeWitt Clinton, the state's leading canal proponent, and other notables entered the canal on that memorable day to begin a triumphant float eastward. Its ultimate goal was New York City. As the dignitary filled fleet passed along the "Grand Canal," ceremony after propitious ceremony was held in the communities along its shores to appropriately recognize and fête the accomplishment of New Yorkers.

Fittingly, at Albany, the state capital, there "occurred the most elaborate reception yet encountered, a whole day being spent in celebration." A procession that included Clinton, the "Lieutenant Governor, Canal Commissioners, Engineers and Assistants, Judicial Officers of the State and Union, Army and Navy Officers, most of the State Officers, military and commercial societies, and many others" marched to the assembly chamber in the capitol to attend the politically mandatory recognition ceremony. Afterward, the notables adjourned "to the elaborately decorated bridge over the Hudson, upon which tables had been placed to accommodate six hundred guests."[1] This unusual dining platform afforded an advantageous view of the river which would carry the canal boats to their ultimate destination.

The building of the Erie Canal was contemporary with the two administrations of President James Monroe. Monroe's presidency, also known as the "Era of Good Feelings," followed the end of the War of 1812. The three-year conflict with England was viewed by a majority of Americans as conclusively proving that the United States could stand up to a great European power, its former colonial overlord, and win. The feeling of nationalism was running high, and with it the mood to step up the pace of internal expansion that had started before the war. But the treaty with England, ratified in 1815, added no new territory to the United States. As a result,

where there had been 7.2 million people contained in seventeen states and additional territories in 1810, by 1820 more than 9.6 million people inhabited the nation's twenty-three states occupying almost the same amount of land (Florida had been purchased from Spain in 1819). Within the next decade, an additional 3.3 million people were added to the total. Nearly all the population boom was due to natural increase; the massive European migration to the United States was yet to come.

Throughout the 1820s, the United States was still primarily a nation of farmers. The trans-Appalachian west offered sorely needed space for the country's new people and their agricultural occupation. But getting them to the west, and equally important, transporting produce and necessary supplies, presented a monumental problem. The national government was only mildly disposed to providing funds to improve transportation to the interior, and the projects that were financed by Congress proceeded very slowly.

New York had approached Washington for monetary support for its canal undertaking but was refused. This meant that it was up to the state to appropriate the money. Not all New Yorkers were convinced in the beginning that the investment of such a large amount of public money was either wise or necessary. The final total needed to dig the ditch was $7.5 million, an immense sum for the period. Yet, when the Erie Canal was completed (and instantly successful), few New Yorkers were willing to openly question the wisdom of the expenditure, and it was difficult to find anyone who would admit to having been anti-canal.

The canal era had arrived for certain in New York by 1825, and the state's far-flung residents wanted to be near the Erie in order to benefit from its success. This, of course, was not possible, so in a way, the Erie Canal was brought to the people of the interior of the state by many lateral canals. State money was thrown with what appeared to be care-free abandon into the construction of a maze of artificial waterways built to connect the Erie with various points in the interior. But much of the money for other forms of transportation had to be found elsewhere.

In 1825, New York City was, as it is now, New York State's unofficial capital (the official seat of government has been moved to Albany in 1798). The great metropolis at the Hudson's mouth did not contain as large a proportion of the state's people as it does today, yet New York already had become the largest city in the United States. The city's population of 166,806 in 1825 was slightly more than one-tenth the state's total. It was the banking and trade center of the nation's largest state, and the city's capitalists were set on keeping and expanding their commercial lead over other Atlantic port cities.

The Erie Canal's opening was a major gain in the race to dominate trade with the nation's hinterlands. The mighty Erie opened a connection to the interior that could never be seriously challenged by any of the other coastal contenders. The builders of the Erie took advantage of New York's Hudson-Mohawk river route through the Appalachian Mountains. Even though a river pass through the mountains existed nowhere else along the 1,500-mile mountain chain, most of the other port cities tried to emulate the Erie's success.

A waterway was constructed from Philadelphia west to the Ohio River at Pittsburgh. But topography worked against the effort. The route crossed elevations nearly four times as high as New York's cross-state canal route, which led to construction costs double those of the Erie. This Pennsylvania Main Line Canal never proved equal to the Erie. Baltimore merchants put their money into the Chesapeake and Ohio Canal being built next to the Potomac River west across Maryland toward the Appalachians. The mountains again proved a formidable barrier, and the Ohio River never was reached. Richmond's hopes were pinned on the James River Canal. Even under the direction of the renowned Benjamin Wright, this westward reach, too, was halted by the mountains.

New York had an advantage that others found impossible to overcome. The east-flowing Mohawk River carved a thousand-foot-deep cut through the Appalachians, from mid-state more than 100 miles to the Hudson. From the Mohawk west to Lake Erie, the remaining 200 miles crossed the level Lake Ontario plain. This topographic blessing helped make the mighty Erie Canal the transportation monarch of the age. Nevertheless, it was in the shadow of this waterway goliath that a new method of conveyance

made its debut. New York was about to enter the "Age of the Iron Horse."

On December 28, 1825, a newspaper in Schenectady carried an announcement that application was about to be made to the New York State Legislature for the incorporation of a railroad company.[2] The proposed Mohawk and Hudson Railroad Company sought to connect the two important rivers for which the company was named. Actually, the goal of the new business was to provide a shorter route for passengers from Albany to the Erie Canal at Schenectady. Most important was the intent that the railroad would complement, not compete, with the "Grand Canal." To do so, a line would be constructed between the state capitol and Schenectady, sixteen miles to the west.

The proposal was the work of George W. Featherstonhaugh (pronounced *Fen'shaw*), a forty-five-year-old English-born resident of Schenectady County.[3] In an effort to ensure the success of his venture, he enlisted the aid of the "Old Patroon," Stephen Van Rensselaer III. A respected scion of an early Dutch family, Van Rensselaer was a prominent landowner, entrepreneur, and politician of the Albany area whose million-acre estate dated from the seventeenth-century Dutch colony of New Netherlands.

Featherstonhaugh and Van Rensselaer sent their petition for a corporate charter to the state assembly early in 1826. It was referred to a committee consisting of Robert Sanders of Schenectady County, William Seamon of Greene County, and Theodore Sill of Oneida County.[4] Schenectady and Oneida were Mohawk Valley counties; Greene was located on the Hudson south of Albany.

Reporting for the committee, Sill noted the success of England's railroads and predicted a similar future for the enterprise in New York. Apparently the only caution expressed by the committee related to the Erie Canal. It was feared that the opening of the railroad might depress toll income between Albany and Schenectady on the state's recently completed enterprise.[5] In a sense, Sill's observation struck at the heart of Featherstonhaugh's confidence in the success of the proposed railroad. Featherstonhaugh saw the railroad as enhancing canal business: Passengers would benefit by moving directly along a sixteen-mile rail line from Albany to Schenectady, instead of by the circuitous twenty-eight-mile-long canal route. Once in Schenectady, travelers would be expected to board canal boats for their westward journey. Ideally, the railroad would complement the canal business. The only other significant objection to the railroad represented the self-interest of the Albany and Schenectady Turnpike Company. Not surprisingly, it feared the competition.[6]

Some additional concerns were raised in the debate over the railroad bill. The assemblyman representing Albany wanted the terms of the charter narrowed relative to location. The original wording called for the terminus on the Hudson to be within three miles north or south of the city. He felt that unless this was changed to require the railroad to locate in Albany trade could be diverted away from the city. This suggestion was challenged by others who felt the Mohawk and Hudson should locate its line to the river wherever it was most convenient. The requirement did not carry.

Although there were some objections to the railroad incorporation, in retrospect it probably mattered little, since Assembly Speaker Crolius supported the bill and envisioned a future wherein passengers and light freight would be carried by railroads, with the heavier loads transported by canals. He desired "to see the experiment of a rail road tried in this country," especially since "the applicants would be permitted to make the experiment at their own expense."[7] Crolius's backing undoubtedly was valuable, and by the end of March the bill easily passed the assembly. Ratification by the state senate came three weeks later.[8]

The corporate charter gave the Mohawk and Hudson Railroad Company the right to construct a railroad between Albany and Schenectady which could transport passengers or freight "by the power and force of steam, of animals or of any mechanical or other power" that the company chose to employ.[9] The charter named Featherstonhaugh, Van Rensselaer, and Lynde Catlin, a Yale-educated New York City banker, as the commissioners charged with opening the subscription of the initial $300,000 capital stock allowed to the company. Thirty-three men, most of them residents of New York City, bought the $100-par-value shares in the company. Only twelve held 100 shares or more, and their collective interest in the railroad totalled 2,321 shares. Of those twelve, five sold their stock in the Mohawk and Hudson before August 1831, the month that the railroad started operation.[10]

By October 1, 1830, about two months after beginning construction, the company's shares were listed on the New York Exchange. The asking price was 110. An indication of the lively interest in Mohawk and Hudson stock can be found in the price activity prior to the opening of the railroad. In July 1831, the shares were trading as high as 174, and within a month after the line opened for business a high of 196¾ was reached. A corporate decision in September to issue another $200,000 worth of stock brought the price down to below 150 by the end of the month.[11]

By July 27, 1826, three months after the act of incorporation, five directors were elected as called for in the charter. Peter Augustus Jay and Andrew Edmeston joined the three commissioners to make up the first corporate board.[12]

George William Featherstonhaugh.
Library of Congress

Most of the twenty paragraphs of the charter that specified the rights and responsibilities of the company were standard in their allowances and protection. One provision was particularly notable in that it forbade the company from constructing "their single or double rail road or way, across the Erie Canal" unless given written authority by the canal commissioners to do so. The state legislature clearly was protecting its own property and source of income by insuring that this new mode of travel would "not in any degree obstruct transportation upon said canal."[13]

At the time the Mohawk and Hudson's charter was under discussion in the legislature, at least one other company was involved in land transportation between the Hudson and Mohawk rivers. Since 1802, the Albany and Schenectady Turnpike Company had operated a toll road between the two cities but, according to one transportation historian, it "had never been a very lucrative enterprise."[14] This situation likely caused the turnpike company to question chartering a railroad that would challenge its trade position. As a result, the railroad's corporate charter contained a provision protecting the rights granted to the turnpike company. The Mohawk and Hudson franchise instructed the railroad company that when it was necessary to cross a "road or highway," the highway "thus intersected" should be restored "to its former state."[15] The Albany and Schenectady Turnpike Company's operations seemed to be reasonably protected, and it became less active in its opposition to the railroad. At least this was the case during the years

Stephen Van Rensselaer.
Library of Congress

in which the railroad's construction plans failed to materialize.

When the Mohawk and Hudson Railroad was revitalized after its four-year moribund state, the turnpike company promptly took a more active approach toward limiting the impending competition. It moved to meet the railway challenge by extending the turnpike to the Hudson River and deciding to "fight fire with fire"—the toll road corporation sought the right to build its own railroad. In April 1830, the state legislature authorized the Albany and Schenectady Turnpike Company to construct a railway on a portion of its turnpike in Albany County.[16]

The act permitting the turnpike company to enter the railroad business was in direct contravention to the Mohawk and Hudson charter passed by the legislature four years earlier. In 1826, the Mohawk and Hudson was given "sole and exclusive right . . . of constructing, erecting, building, making and using a single or double rail road" from Albany to Schenectady.[17] The conflicting legislation resulted in the two companies expanding the contest between them. Evidence of this can be found in the legislation itself and in the Albany newspapers of the day.

In 1830, the Mohawk and Hudson Railroad Company changed the engineers in charge of construction, and with the change came tangible activity, at last. Increased activity on the part of the railroad company caused the Albany and Schenectady Turnpike Company to hire a civil engineer to advise it on the manner and cost of building a railway upon its turnpike.[18] The turnpike company also petitioned the legislature to extend the company's right to build a railway as far as Schenectady.[19]

The Mohawk and Hudson countered with a petition to the state lawmakers to allow it to build a branch line from the point at which the railroad intersected the Great Western Turnpike, a major route to western New York, to the square in front of the state capitol.[20] Although the legislature acted on neither bill, the Albany and Schenectady managed to increase its capital stock by $400,000 in order to construct the railroad authorized by the act of 1830. The company sought to raise even more money by a levy of $20 on each share already issued.

These moves on the part of the turnpike company caught the attention of the railroad corporation. The Mohawk and Hudson directors requested a meeting with representatives of the Albany and Schenectady. The meeting took place in October 1831, with Churchill C. Cambreling, Lynde Catlin, and John DeGraff representing the railroad company. Within a month, an agreement was concluded that formed the basis for legislation passed the following April.[21]

The act reflected the compromise worked out between the two transportation companies. The Mohawk and Hudson received approval to build a line from its intersection with the Great Western pike to Capitol Square and could increase its capital by $100,000. The additional stock would be available for purchase, at par, by the stockholders of the Albany and Schenectady in shares of $100 each. If an individual shareholder did not take up the offer made in proportion to the shares held in the turnpike company, then the company itself could purchase the Mohawk and Hudson shares.[22] When the block of new stock was put up for purchase on June 5, the entire amount was subscribed within four days, apparently all taken by turnpike shareholders.[23]

Although the major provisions of the pact between the two companies seemed to proceed without problem, evidently one portion proved difficult. The act of April 2, 1832, called for the Mohawk and Hudson to run its line from Capitol Square easterly to the Albany basin.[24] Yet, although the Capitol Square branch was completed by January 1, 1833, the extension to the basin was not under construction. A survey for the route had been done, but no action was taken. On July 19, representatives of the railroad met with the president of the Albany and Schenectady Turnpike Company in order to get the turnpike company to consent to a change in the agreement. The Mohawk and Hudson leadership desired to

abandon the Albany basin branch and to build an alternate route from the river, instead. The preferred line would run "from near the foot of the eastern inclined plane through Court, Market, and Quay Streets to State Street or as much further along Quay Street as may be deemed useful."[25]

As Stevens pointed out in his history, the Mohawk and Hudson directors wanted out of their agreement with the Albany and Schenectady Turnpike Company to build a branch line to the Albany basin. The railway directors adopted a resolution that would provide for an alternate route if the Albany and Schenectady leadership consented to drop the basin requirement.[26] But the turnpike company did not allow an alteration of the agreement, and a direct rail line was built from Capitol Square, down State Street to the basin at the Hudson River.[27]

Even though the railroad company constructed the connection to the river via State Street in order to avoid breach of contract with the turnpike company, the railroad did not escape legal problems. For that matter, the railroad also failed to dodge public outcry. The Mohawk and Hudson Board of Directors had instructed the engineer to run the survey for the line down the lower portion of State Street in May 1833. Work apparently was well under way by summer, since reactions to the line construction began to appear in the press.

In late July, a brief letter was published in the *Gazette* praising the mayor of Albany for forbidding the construction of a double rail on the city streets. According to the writer, a single track "is a great nuisance, the other would be intolerable."[28] Albany mayor Francis Bloodgood entered into the fray and took direct action to prevent the installation of more than one track on State Street hill between Capitol Square and the Albany basin on the Hudson River. He defended his activity, which included ordering the arrest of some Mohawk and Hudson workmen, in a lengthy statement. The mayor asserted that his move was necessary because the railroad had exceeded its authority in attempting to construct an extra track on State Street east of the capitol park. He concluded that, in the end, the matter would be up to the state legislature to settle.[29]

The outcry against the railroad did not cease as the completion of the basin branch neared. Near the end of November, the Albany Common Council supported the mayor with a resolution explaining that, although the council had previously granted permission to the Mohawk and Hudson to use such streets as might be necessary in constructing their approved line, State Street from Capitol Square to the basin was too steep to be useful for a railroad. Therefore, the railroad company should stop taking up pavement on State Street.[30] A few days later, a letter appeared from "Amicus" that backed the action the city fathers took relative to the infamous branch. The penman cautioned that "it is always impolitic and even dangerous for an incorporated company to disregard public feeling, and the moment they discover they have done so, they should change their course."[31] This warning was in reaction to the railroad company's taking land apparently regarded as public property. A final admonition contained in the statement related to the agreement with the turnpike company. Amicus scolded, "if they [the Mohawk and Hudson] feel themselves unreasonably pushed by the Albany and Schenectady Turnpike company then let them forthwith seek another route."[32] One can only wonder what connection "Amicus" may have had with the turnpike enterprise.

The issue of the Capitol Square to Albany basin branch stretched out for another eighteen months until finally, in June 1835, the Mayor's Court of Albany cited as a nuisance the lower State Street part of the railroad and ordered it removed. The Mohawk and Hudson, on advice from counsel, took no immediate action. Three months passed before a second resolution on the part of the mayor's court moved the company to defend its inactivity. The Mohawk and Hudson attempted to hide behind the agreement with the Albany and Schenectady, and claimed that taking up the track would open them to suit from the turnpike people. The mayor's court avoided potential litigation between the companies by ordering the sheriff to take up the line. The railroad company was fined $350, the estimated cost of the work, plus $30 in fees. The sheriff then hired the railroad company to remove the track, apparently in lieu of payment of the fine.[33] This finally ended nearly a decade of relationship between the two land transportation companies. Once the railroad company moved ahead in earnest to construct its line, the turnpike company, after putting up a limited fight, decided to come to terms with the competitor that threatened to put its toll road out of business.

Finally, the Mohawk and Hudson Railroad Company began its new addition to New York's transportation network. In this novel form of land conveyance called a railroad, the capitalists of New York City, who profited so much by the building of the Erie Canal, saw another opportunity in their race against the other major coastal cities for the domination of inland trade. They bought most of the stock in the Mohawk and Hudson and dominated the company's board of directors. Notably missing among the early directors were significant numbers of investors from New York's capital district. Perhaps the locals lacked faith in the ability of the railroad to compete with the canal, or maybe they simply lacked the money and competitive drive of the entrepreneurs at the other end of the Hudson.

John Jacob Astor
Library of Congress

III: Construction

As the expanding transportation network in the state of New York was about to change with the addition of its first railroad, the state and the nation also were undergoing changes other than those relative to the movement of people and goods. The "Era of Good Feeling," with its accompanying nationalistic impulse, was on the wane. It was being replaced by a rise in sectionalism. The presidential election of 1824 exemplified this transition.

In 1820, when James Monroe ran for a second term, he was, for all intents, the only candidate. His party, the Democratic-Republican, was the overwhelmingly predominant political party. By 1824, there were four candidates in the race for the presidency, all claiming to be members of the same party. One candidate was from the Northeast, one was from the South, and two were from the then western states of Kentucky and Tennessee. The campaign was so tumultuous and the vote so split that the contest landed in the House of Representatives, whose members would decide the outcome. The two candidates who had received the most votes were John Quincy Adams from Massachusetts and Andrew Jackson from Tennessee. As a result of a near frenzy of "wheeling and dealing," Adams emerged with the presidency, but the supporters of "Old Hickory" vowed revenge for what they perceived as an injustice for Jackson, who actually had won the most popular votes.

One of the results of the election of 1824 was the fractionalizing of the old Democratic-Republican Party of Thomas Jefferson into two parties—the National Republicans, who supported Adams, and the Democrats, who stood behind Jackson. When the major contest between the two men and their parties occurred in the presidential race of 1828, Jackson won.

When Jackson entered the White House in 1829, one of his allies entered the governor's mansion in New York State. Governor Martin Van Buren's star had been rising throughout the decade of the 1820s. Aided by the adoption of a new state constitution in 1821, Van Buren began his climb toward his ultimate political goal—the presidency— which he achieved in 1836. New York's Constitution of 1821 reformed the franchise in the state and, in doing so, potentially increased voter numbers and voter ability to participate in the political process. It also markedly added to the power of the governor. Van Buren capitalized on this and built a political machine known as the "Albany Regency" to assist him in his drive to power. Although he and the "Regency" had not backed Jackson in 1824, by 1828 they had climbed on Jackson's bandwagon.

The changes that took place in the state and the nation during the 1820s were not limited to politics, although many were inextricably linked with the proliferation of political parties and the inter-party squabbles that followed. Reform assumed many different shapes. Among the various changes that were attempted or became reality were educational reform, penal reform, temperance, women's rights, the abolition of slavery, and economic reform. The latter was, to no small extent, encouraged by the continuing industrialization in the United States. Political parties were not immune from the reform movements; they were an integral part of the phenomena and their platforms reflected their respective stands.

New York was among the leaders in the spreading revolution in business and industry. This made sense for a state with the largest population, an abundance of excellent navigable natural waterways and the new Erie Canal, plenty of rushing streams to provide water power, vast forests for firewood, a modicum of mineral resources, and New York City's wonderful port and significant accumulation of capital. New York's industrial growth also affected the growth and divergence of its political parties.

It was against such a backdrop of change that the germ of the idea for the first railroad in New York, which occurred in 1825 and began to take root in 1826, grew very slowly. But, while the New York company and its engineer continued to plan and discuss, elsewhere others moved ahead. The first railroad to successfully utilize steam power in the United States commenced service in 1830. This was the Charleston and Hamburg Railroad, which eventually ran across 130 miles of South Carolina. The line was engineered by Horatio Allen, who had assisted John B. Jervis on the Delaware and Hudson's gravity railroad. South Carolina's locomotive leadership was quickly challenged, first by the Baltimore and Ohio, which opened for business in May 1830 using horsepower, and then thirteen months later using locomotive power, and next by New York's Mohawk and Hudson.

These railroads may have taken the lead, but their monopoly was quickly put in jeopardy. By 1832, twenty-five railroads had applied for corporate charters in New York State alone. Within eight years, twenty-two of the twenty-six states had railroads. By then, New York was second in the nation in total mileage with 374, but this was only half of the track length that Pennsylvania already had put down.[1]

Among the results of this railroad-building boom was the increased and constant demand for skilled civil engineers. This phenomenon was made problematic by the simultaneous call for experienced engineers to direct construction of the proliferating canals—after all, railroads as yet had not overtaken canals as the ideal method of inexpensive transportation.

The completion of the Erie Canal doubled the number of trained American civil engineers. But these men, along with the graduates of the United States Military Academy at West Point, were practically the only domestic engineers with sufficient training to meet the rapidly expanding need. As a result, those engineers who acquired a high reputation were almost constantly sought for their building skills. They tended to move from project to project with an amazing frequency, looking for commissions that would be challenging and would enhance their reputations. Perhaps this is what inspired Peter Fleming, the Mohawk and Hudson's initial civil engineer, to leave his post in late 1829.

Fleming was selected to direct the building of the Mohawk and Hudson in June 1826 at an annual salary of $1,500.[2] His three-and-one-half year tenure evidently was preoccupied with planning, since no actual construction got underway. Apparently, the lack of activity between 1826 and 1828 was not his fault. George Featherstonhaugh referred to one of the problems at the end of 1826 in a letter written from Scarborough, England, to Theodore Sill, a member of the New York State Assembly. While Featherstonhaugh was in England, he met with Peter Fleming, who had been sent there by the company to gather information on English railroads.

In his correspondence to Sill, Featherstonhaugh complained about the fifteenth and seventeenth paragraphs of the act of incorporation.[3] The fifteenth provision stated "that the stockholders and directors of the said corporation shall be . . . personally liable for payment of all debts contracted by the said corporation or by their agents." The seventeenth paragraph gave the legislature a five-year option after completion of the railroad, during which time if the lawmakers chose to reimburse the company for its construction costs, "the said rail road shall vest in and become the property of the people of this state."[4] In other words, the directors and stockholders would not be shielded by a corporate charter that treated the corporation as a legal body by limiting liability. In addition, the state could at anytime during the first five years of railroad operation take possession of the company.

In January 1827, the Mohawk and Hudson petitioned the legislature for removal of the onerous charter provisions. On January 23, a legislative committee, consisting of Alonzo Paige of Schenectady County, Francis Granger of Ontario County, and John Haswell of Albany County, reported that it was "convinced that the prayer of the petitioners ought to be granted."[5] The fact that a majority of the committee represented Mohawk and Hudson counties may have influenced the decision. In any case, no legislative action was taken in 1827. It was not until March 28, 1828, after Featherstonhaugh returned from England and personally took charge of the campaign, that the amending legislation passed. The legislature granted the company more or less its request by limiting director liability, altering its own prerogative to take possession of the railway, and increasing the number of corporate directors to nine, as favored by the company.[6] Now the way was clear for construction to begin.

Once appointed the company's engineer, Peter Fleming moved with remarkable alacrity and had his initial cost estimate for construction completed by late July 1826. Adding the usual ten percent for "contingencies," the engineer estimated twenty miles of railroad could be built for a total of $343,425, or roughly $17,000 per mile. Fleming's figure included beam timber at $12 per 100 feet, and iron rails and chairs to hold the rails to the beams at $65 per ton.[7] The engineer's calculation was nearly double the per-mile estimate made by Featherstonhaugh a year earlier.[8] It was not until early 1829 that Fleming presented another cost estimate, after the charter problems had been corrected.

In January 1829, the new corporate board consisting of nine directors[9] named Featherstonhaugh, John Jacob Astor, and Lynde Catlin to a committee charged with taking steps to start construction of the Mohawk and Hudson Railroad. The February 12 edition of the New York *Daily Advertiser* reported that the prospect of this long-delayed project was now a certainty. It was noted that the report of Peter Fleming, "concurred in by Benjamin Wright, to whom it and the surveys were submitted," was accepted by the board of directors.[10] Perhaps it was the imprimatur of the highly esteemed Wright that prompted the Albany *Gazette* to confidently predict shortly thereafter that construction would commence in the spring along the route into south Albany. The news of the building of a new river dock was disclosed, along with speculation that a railroad soon would be built between Albany and Boston.[11]

Ten days before the *Gazette*'s predictions, the company directors received the select committee report, along with Fleming's raised calculations. This time the engineer's total for 16.2 miles of railway was $275,366.29, or slightly less than $17,000 per mile. As it turned out, the actual per-mile cost was $15,531.87, compared with $15,149 in Fleming's 1826 estimate. In calculating the per-mile construction cost, the engineer factored in, among other materials, 7,040 cubic feet of oak beams at 25 cents a cubic foot, 1¼-inch oak top planking at $2.50 per 100 feet, and iron rail for four lines at $4 per yard.

The board acted upon the information immediately, authorized Featherstonhaugh to let the necessary contracts, and instructed treasurer Catlin to levy a call of $3 per share upon the stockholders to be paid on April 1.[12] Featherstonhaugh moved with equal speed, as evidenced by a notice that appeared on February 27 calling for bids on 150,000 cubic feet of white oak, 8 inches by 7 inches, in lengths of 12 feet 2 inches, 15 feet 2 inches and 18 feet 2 inches; 12,000 cubic feet of white oak 8 inches by 4 inches by 13 feet long; 700,000 feet of white oak plank 4½ inches by 1½ inches thick with 1-inch bevel; 350,000 feet of hemlock plank 9 inches by 3 inches by 13 feet long; 350,000 feet of elm plank; and 423,000 feet of red beech. Featherstonhaugh specified that he needed to know not only the geographic location of the timber, but also whether it grew on lowland or upland.[13]

With this activity, the Mohawk and Hudson Railroad finally was underway—or maybe not.

When the Mohawk and Hudson Board of Directors met on March 13, 1829, in New York City, Van Rensselaer, Featherstonhaugh, and Duane were not present. Curiously, the six members in attendance reversed some of the important resolutions passed at the February meeting. They suspended the previously authorized contracts for materials and for preliminary construction, and they lowered the $3 per share assessment to $1 per share. Thereafter, little new business was conducted until the election of a new board on May 25.

At the meeting of the new corporate board on July 14, Van Rensselaer was again named president, Nicholas Fish became vice president and James Renwick, a new member from New York City, took the secretary's position. A week later, Catlin was continued as treasurer. An inquiry was sent to the still-absent George Featherstonhaugh to determine his intentions in regard to serving as a director.

The founder's reply came ten days later in the form of his resignation, effective August 1. Churchill C. Cambreling, a New York City politician, was elected to replace him. Featherstonhaugh severed his remaining connection with the company by the end of November when he offered his 601 shares, totalling slightly more than one-fifth of the Mohawk and Hudson capital stock, to the company and moved to Philadelphia. Perhaps the loss of his wife in June 1828, followed by the complete destruction by fire of his Duanesburgh mansion a year later, drove him to seek a new life in the "City of Brotherly Love."[14]

George W. Featherstonhaugh's departure from the railroad company that was his brainchild was followed by several months of what could be described as a lack of direction. The board instructed engineer Fleming to draw up plans for locomotives, stationary engines for the two inclined planes, and other such machinery and materials necessary to move passengers and freight. He also was to submit the route plan, which, of course, already had been done. Nevertheless, Fleming did as charged and made his report on September 22. Three days later, a stockholders meeting took place with only fifteen of the forty shareholders present. Little was accomplished, except that significant action on Fleming's report was put off until the next meeting. By the time the subsequent assembly took place, two directors had resigned. Only ten stockholders attended the meeting on November 7, but they were in complete agreement that the board of directors should "take decisive measures to carry the objects of this incorporation into effect."[15]

The company owners, or at least those who were at the November 7 meeting, were adamant that the railroad should be built. Unfortunately, they were soon faced with yet another block to the road's progress: When the directors met on January 8, 1830, they were greeted by Peter Fleming's letter of resignation. The news should have come as no surprise, since he already had left company employ.[16] At the time of Fleming's resignation, a little more than four years had passed since the notice of the railroad's incorporation intent had appeared in the Schenectady *Cabinet*, and no real progress had been made in actually building the Mohawk and Hudson.

Fleming's departure must have seemed the final blow to the struggling railroad company, at least to the desperate directors. Actually, Fleming's resignation opened a window of opportunity. In their search for a replacement, the company directors found not only a very competent engineer, but one who had genuine experience in railroad construction. Fleming's successor was John Bloomfield Jervis.

When Jervis was offered the Mohawk and Hudson appointment in March 1830, he was still chief engineer of the Delaware and Hudson Canal. It was unquestionably his Delaware and Hudson employment that landed him the New York railroad job. James Renwick, the Mohawk and Hudson's corporate secretary, also was a consultant for the canal company. In fact, Renwick was the person to whom Jervis's report on the Carbondale railway was submitted for review in the fall of 1827. Renwick thus became acquainted with Jervis's engineering skills, particularly as they applied to railroads. The two men became friends, with great respect for each other's ability. Evidence of this can be found in the fact that in 1830, Renwick, a professor of science at Columbia, asked Jervis's opinion on the wisdom of offering a civil engineering course at the college.[17]

John B. Jervis at about 40 years of age.
Courtesy of the Jervis Library, Rome, New York

Renwick, as company secretary, invited Jervis to accept the Mohawk and Hudson employ at a salary of $2,000 for half-time (alternating months) work for the first year. Annualized, this was more than two and a half times the yearly amount paid to Fleming. Jervis was in the service of the Delaware and Hudson Canal Company at the time and remained so until May 1830, but he did not hesitate in moving ahead on the Mohawk and Hudson, and he selected two resident engineers to assist him less than a week after his own acceptance. Jervis offered John Clark, an engineer on the Delaware and Hudson Canal, one of the positions; the other went to Jervis's younger brother, Timothy, an experienced civil engineer. The senior Jervis assured Renwick that this was the reason for hiring his brother and that doing so was not a conflict of interest.

Interesting insight into Jervis's lack of regard for army engineers can be found in his letter offering the position to John Clark. Jervis mentioned that some of the Mohawk and Hudson directors suggested asking for assistance from the U.S. Army Corps of Engineers "to obtain the benefit of their scientific aid." Jervis felt the majority on the board was against doing so and the new chief engineer concurred, since he was "decidedly against committing the execution of such work to such men."[18] Jervis was not any more explicit about his lack of trust in the ability of the corps of engineers.

As soon as the organization of his engineering party was complete, Jervis began the preliminary survey of the railroad route. He could recommend the line, but its final approval was up to a committee comprised of John Jacob Astor, Lynde Catlin, and James Renwick. According to a contemporary account of the building of the Mohawk and Hudson, the Jervis route "was generally three fourths of a mile north of Mr. Fleming's line except at the two terminations. It is believed that no part of Mr. Fleming's plan has been adopted."[19]

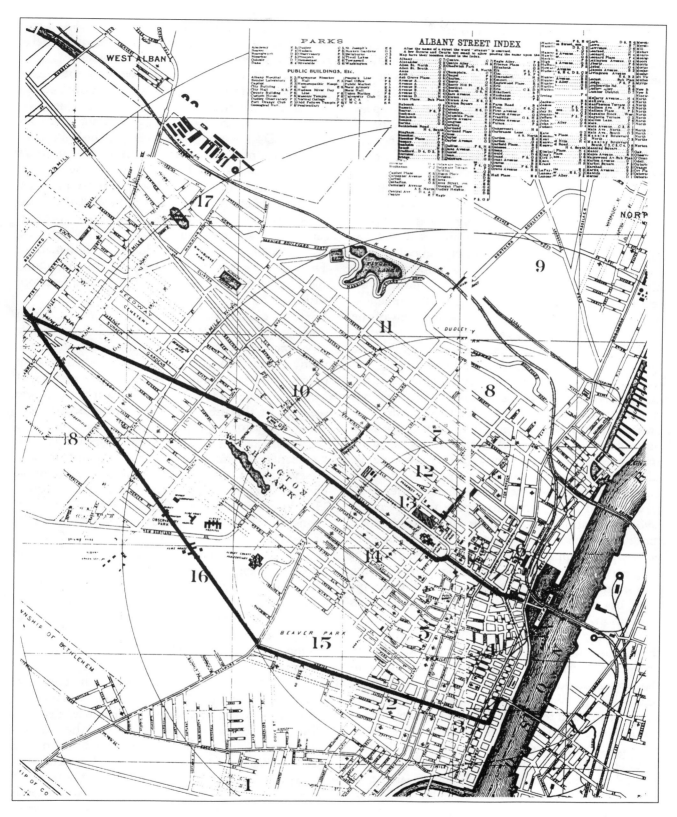

Black lines on this 1910 Albany map indicate the original route of the
Mohawk and Hudson Railroad, including the State Street branch.

The proposed line ran a straight sixteen miles, terminating at the Hudson River at Gansevoort Street in Albany at its eastern end, and at Mill Street near the original Erie Canal in Schenectady at the western end. As usual, Jervis moved rapidly; by mid-July 1830 he had completed a twenty-two page report to the company. The meticulously prepared document described the materials to be used in track construction, the manner in which the track would be laid, and a detailed breakdown of cost estimates.[20]

In selecting white pine for the rail timber, Jervis noted that it and the manner in which it would be secured to the stone blocks (using cast iron braces) would result in a twelve-year life span for the timbers. Replacement costs would average only about $750 to $800 per mile of single rail.[21] Jervis considered several kinds of wood before settling on white pine. In his report he discussed the merits of oak, tamarack, hemlock, and southern yellow pine in terms of the strength, durability, and tendency of each to warp, spring, and check. He cited the experience of the Quincy, Baltimore and Ohio, and Carbondale railroads in terms of their respective timber rails, the extent to which each supported loads of various weights, and the degree to which the loads compressed the iron strips or bars into the wooden rails. Jervis found many desirable properties in tamarack and, although he decided in favor of white pine, he admitted "indulging some hope that the Tamarack may on further Enquiry [sic] be found preferable." Jervis found southern yellow pine to have many favorable qualities, but he rejected its use based upon the "deception said to be practised [sic] by dealers" in yellow pine—apparently they had the reputation of frequently "delivering a timber so closely resembling [southern yellow pine] as to make it difficult for those not much accustomed to its use to detect its imposition."[22]

Most of the railroad would be constructed with the timber rails resting on stone blocks. But an alternative method of support was used for rails crossing embankments. In order to help maintain the road's level, embankments of sand, clay, or loam were constructed to cross major depressions. Due to the different lengths of time it took for each fill material to settle properly, Jervis decided the rails would rest on posts "sunk about 4 feet and resting on a piece of 2 inch plank 12 by 18 inches laid in the bottom of the shaft." A cross sill would be placed on top of the posts and "treenailed into the head; the sills to have a notch or joggle joint cut in each end to receive the rails."[23] It was estimated that the five

miles, eight chains of railroad on posts would cost about $1,500 a mile less than the remaining twelve miles and seventeen chains on stone blocks.[24]

As to the width of the road between the tracks, Jervis admitted to being in a quandary about chosing between 5 feet and 4 feet 9 inches. Here again he turned to the practice of existing railroads. The Carbondale (D&H Gravity) Railroad that he built had a track gauge of 4 feet 3 inches, while the Baltimore and Ohio used 4 feet 9¼ inches. Both the Quincy road in Massachusetts and South Carolina's Charleston and Hamburg used 5 feet as the width between tracks. After weighing the pros and cons of the two gauges he was considering, he decided to put off a decision pending obtaining additional information. The difference would not affect the width of grading, and therefore would not hold up the start of construction.[25]

Jervis did not finalize his choice of a 4 feet 9 inch track gauge until November. By then it was necessary, since he was making decisions concerning locomotives and their dimensions. He studied English practice and found railroads there were between 4 feet 6 inches and 4 feet 8½ inches "clear between the tracks." At the time he also, perhaps unwittingly, made a plea for track gauge standardization. Jervis suggested that his company's directors inform the Camden and Amboy Railroad Company in New Jersey of the gauge that the Mohawk and Hudson had chosen "in order to induce them to adopt the same." His objective was not to achieve rolling stock interchangeability for the two widely separated railroads, but was based on Jervis's reasoning that the Camden and Amboy was being constructed "essentially for passengers, and [was] in the vicinity of those establishments [in New York City] that may with equal convenience furnish carriages and engines for both [railroads]."[26] There is no evidence to indicate that Jervis had a financial interest in any of "those establishments," but he certainly was well acquainted with persons who had invested in them.

The chief engineer recommended the construction of a "McAdamized" horse path between the rails after the railroad was completed. Jervis reasoned that although locomotives were to be used, there might be instances, due to the "slippery condition of the rails by reason of their being covered with frost[,] snow[,] or sleet and the temporary use of horses will be necessary." He noted that the "road will also be improved in firmness by this measure" and warned the railroad's board of directors that "it would not be prudent to neglect the construction of a horse path."[27]

Nine of the twenty-two pages of Jervis's report to the board of directors contained cost estimates. The entire expense of grading he calculated at $83,188.57. The road's thirteen culverts would total $9,769.91, or an average of slightly more than $750 each for structures built of limestone masonry and planking.[28] The twenty-one bridges, mostly farm spans, were figured to cost a total of $1,629. The most expensive was the Pearl Street bridge in Albany, at $475. In addition to the expenditure for bridges, $2,815 was added for 3,312 rods of fencing.

Jervis included $9,600 for 48,000 cubic feet of rail timber, and $19,305 for the 351 tons of iron he reckoned would be needed for eighteen miles of road. Another $1,800 was included for spikes to secure the iron, and $4,000 for the friction rollers for the two inclined planes. To this amount was added $5,400 for labor to install the rail iron. Also, the fifteen miles of McAdamized horse path would cost an estimated $6,000. In all, the chief engineer submitted a construction estimate amounting to $215,661.12 for the Mohawk and Hudson Railroad.[29]

Although there seems to be some disagreement as to the exact date of ground breaking for the railroad construction, S. DeWitt Bloodgood, an Albany resident who was corresponding secretary for the Albany Institute, wrote that it occurred on August 12, 1830. The event took place in Schenectady and was marked by an address given by "C[hurchill] C. Cambreling, Esq. who throughout the whole work has proved a persevering and efficient agent of the Company."[30] At last, construction started, more than four and one half years after the initial notice of the new company had appeared. Since George Featherstonhaugh made the announcement in a Schenectady newspaper, it was fitting that the ground-breaking ceremony took place in that community.

The building of the Mohawk and Hudson Railroad moved ahead rapidly and routinely, and within a year, twelve miles of single track had been completed. The sandy plain between Albany and Schenectady across which the railway was laid was described by Jervis as " a table land of fair character for a good line and easy grades." The principal obstructions to the rapid completion of the entire line were the two steep approach grades to the level area between the two cities. They were inclines of "near[ly] two hundred feet [in elevation] from the Hudson and over one hundred feet from the Mohawk."[31] The inclines ran from the intersection of Morton Street and Delaware Avenue in Albany to the Hudson River, and from the top of the Crane Street hill in Schenectady to the level of the Mohawk River.[32] The planes were constructed on an angle that was one foot in rise for eighteen feet of horizontal.[33]

Horses were considered for the motive power on the inclines, but the chief engineer favored the use of stationary steam engines, which would be more economical for heavier loads and could be used with a higher degree of safety in lowering the carriages down the plane.[34] Railroad cars were raised and lowered on the inclined planes attached to ropes five and one-quarter inches in circumference. At the Albany

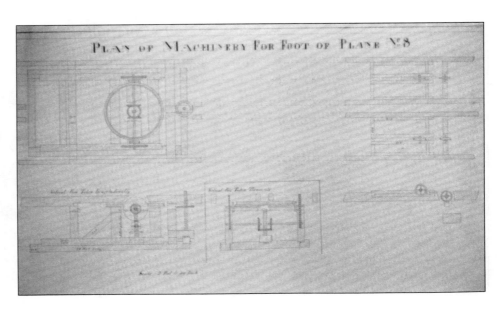

Inclined plane machinery, Delaware & Hudson gravity railroad.

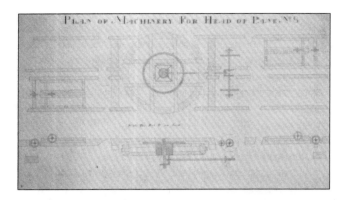

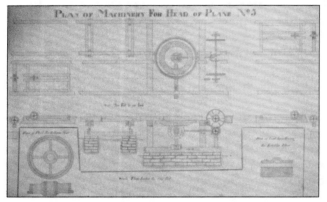

plane, 3,480 feet of rope were needed; 2,210 feet were required at Schenectady.[35] The ropes were attached to stationary, twelve-horsepower, high-pressure steam engines having two cylinders, seven and a half inches by twenty-six inches. The "shackle bars are connected with an axis on the extremity of which is a crown wheel, working with another at right angles, on a shaft placed vertically" the upper end of "which is near the surface of the road and directly in its centre, a larger wheel around the circumference of which the hauling ropes pass, and run on rollers placed at regular distances down the plane."[36]

To Jervis, the use of the stationary steam engines was in keeping with the prevailing theories pertaining to locomotive tractive power. Construction of a railroad on steep inclines "at that day was regarded as impractical without the planes with stationary

Left: Inclined plane machinery, Delaware and Hudson gravity railroad. Courtesy of the Jervis Collection

Below: Plan for all-iron rail as proposed by Jervis. Courtesy of the Jervis Collection

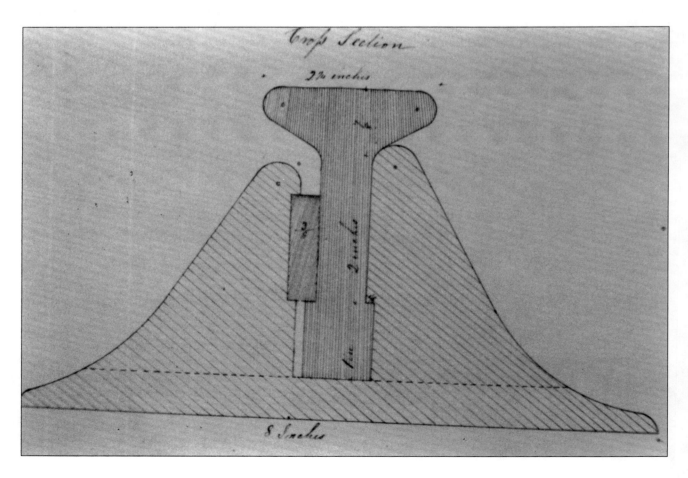

power."[37] According to Jervis, an alternate route that might have resulted in the elimination of the need for the inclined planes met with strong opposition from citizens of Albany who objected to a railroad through the heart of the city.[38]

While work was progressing on the roadbed and track, Jervis made a suggestion to the company directors that was influenced by his less-than-successful Delaware and Hudson experience. He posed the possibility of the future adoption of an all-iron rail instead of the wooden rail with an iron cap. To prepare for this, he recommended that the stone blocks supporting the wooden rails, or stringers, be spaced three feet apart instead of four, which would provide improved support for the heavier rail. The chief engineer favored the change even though it would add approximately $1,100 per mile to the cost of the road construction. Jervis apprised the railroad directors of his opinion on the iron rail the day before he received correspondence from Renwick on the same subject. Renwick wrote that the use of all-iron rail was being considered by the directors and that they had delayed action on the "proper form" for a rail until a meeting with Jervis could be arranged. The meeting held in John Jacob Astor's office in New York City produced no immediate change in the original rail plan, but it was decided to space the rail support blocks closer together. And, as Jervis earlier had planned, the iron rail caps were set 4 feet 9 inches apart (4 feet 8½ inches currently is standard track gauge in the United States).[39]

A little more than a year later, in October 1831, Jervis elaborated on the subject of the iron rail in a nine-page letter to Churchill C. Cambreling. The correspondence was prompted by Cambreling's request for some comparisons between the cost of wooden versus all-iron rails. Jervis referred to the experience of other railroads, including the Liverpool and Manchester, factored in the weight of newer and heavier locomotives, and referred to the chief trade of the railroad at that time. The "character of the passenger business" is one that "demands the least practical interruption. The expectations of the public have been so much excited in reference to rapid traveling (and that must be by locomotive steam power) that they will not be satisfied with moderate speed say 10 or 12 miles per hour. They must have 15 as a regular business." Jervis then typically pointed to economy in reminding Cambreling that "larger engines may be used on an iron road with very little increase of their daily expense, and will therefore be more economical for the work they do than those which must be used on a timber rail."[40]

Having pointed out the benefit of iron rails with heavier locomotives, Jervis tried another ploy to win Cambreling over with reference to the company's new English machine. Timber was not a "suitable material for rails where so great a weight is put on it," as was the case with the English import. Although the rails did not break, "the wood compresses under the plate and this will eventually destroy the timber." Jervis professed no doubt that "without iron rails...we shall have to abandon the use of the English engine."[41]

Jervis recommended the company directors authorize iron rail for the Mohawk and Hudson's second track. He discussed the relative merits of both English elliptical rail and the parallel rail manufactured in that country. He quoted a Mr. Hartley, "the engineer of the Liverpool docks" and "of great celebrity" as favoring the parallel rail "as the most economical for the same strength." Jervis reasoned that it was "proper to consult the experience of English engineers on this subject."[42] He included an illustration of the rail that he favored in the letter to Cambreling. Per mile, the parallel type of iron rail would cost: $2,564.10 for fifty-five tons of rail; $800 for twenty tons of cast iron chairs; $120 for the required 3,000 pounds of spikes; and $140 for 3,500 pounds of keys for the chairs. Jervis added to the total $1,812.05 for freight, insurance, foreign exchange, and a 50 percent duty on the imported rails. The result was $2,432.06 more for a mile of all-iron rail over the cost for the same distance of wooden rail with iron plates. The difference for the 13.9 miles of the all-iron second track between the inclined planes in Albany and Schenectady was estimated at $33,805.63.[43]

Perhaps the most important part of the Jervis letter to Cambreling was the engineer's suggestion that on the sand embankments it would be advisable to put "down iron rails on Wooden cross sleepers."[44] This was Jervis's first reference to the use of wood cross ties, and perhaps was the pioneer statement on what would become common practice in railroad construction.

Apparently, Cambreling was not convinced of the need for the more expensive iron rails. He wrote Jervis that he had "examined wooden rails [on the Baltimore and Ohio Railroad]...to see whether iron has been driven into the wood but I cannot perceive that the slightest impression has been made. I saw cars and loads of 8-10 tons each on 4 wheels." Cambreling admitted, however, that even though heavy freight

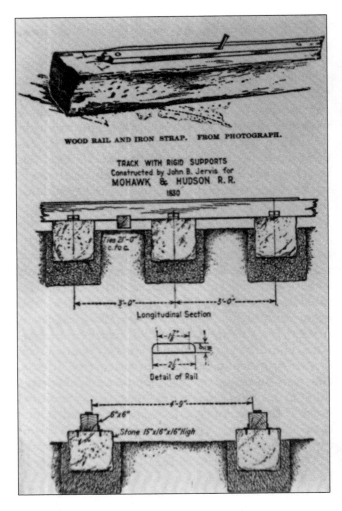

Track construction.
From Stevens, *New York Central*

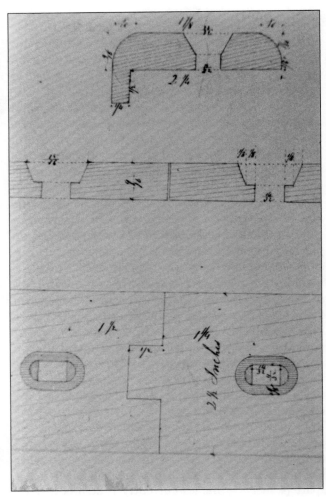

Detail of iron strap rail that was fastened to wooden
stringers. Courtesy of the Jervis Collection

cars were used "constantly," locomotives were "only
occasionally used."[45]

Thus ended Jervis's push for an all-iron rail for
the Mohawk and Hudson Railroad. The Mohawk
and Hudson's rails continued to be constructed of
white and Norway pine topped by the approximately two inch by one-half inch iron caps, or strips.
For a time, immediate savings won out over the
far-sighted wisdom of a chief engineer who recognized the benefits of iron rails and realized that they
would be universally adopted in the future—the
increasingly heavier locomotives would necessitate
doing so.

Once the engineering parties finished the survey
and staked out the route, the initial stage of railroad
construction involved grading. The line was divided
into thirty sections in order to expedite the grading,
making each section an average of one-half mile in

length. The composition of the earth along the right-
of-way was mainly sand with some clay. Contractors
were allowed between seven and eight cents per cubic
yard to move sand, and nine to eleven cents per cubic
yard for the clay. The so-called two-way method of
payment was used when, in order to keep the track
level, material was excavated from elevations along
the route and placed in nearby embankments being
built across several ravines. That is, a unit price was
established for the estimated amount of material to
be moved.[46]

Bloodgood described the work that followed the
grading. Along each line of rails, square holes large
enough to hold nine cubic feet of broken stone were
dug three feet apart on center; when the holes were
dug in clay they were "connected by a neck." The
stone fill was broken into pieces about two inches in
diameter before being placed in the holes. This

formed the foundation upon which the stone block rail supports were placed, which were "quarried either on the canal twelve miles above Schenectady, or at Sing Sing on the Hudson." The blocks, roughly sixteen inches on a side, were "dressed on the upper side only, but have a flat bottom in order to lie evenly upon the broken stone." After the stone blocks were placed in the holes, "a massive wooden pounder, with four arms, managed by the united strength of four men, is applied, to bring them exactly to their level" in the broken stone.[47]

Once the stone blocks were set and levelled, holes were drilled in the top of the block "and by means of a simple adaptation of an old principle...four holes can be drilled at once,"[48] which saved time and labor. Wooden plugs about four inches long and an inch in diameter, made from slow-to-rot locust, were placed in the holes. Iron spikes used to hold down the rail chairs were driven into the locust plugs. The cast iron chairs intended to hold the rails to the stone were either single or double. The double chairs crossed underneath the rail and held it on both sides, while the single chairs supported only one side of the rail. Double chairs were "used in the proportion of one to three single chairs."[49]

The pine rails were twenty to twenty-four feet long and six inches square. Once placed in the chairs, they were trued with wooden wedges driven on the outside of the rail. Since the two wood rails that formed the principal basis of the railroad track were not held together using cross-ties or sleepers, spacing pieces placed twenty-one feet apart were used to keep the rails parallel.

Atop the pine rails were laid English wrought iron rails imported from Wolverhampton, Staffordshire. These iron rails, two and one-half inches wide at the base rounded to one and seven-eighths inches at the top were nine-sixteenth of an inch thick and weighed twenty-one tons to the mile. The wrought iron strips were secured to the wooden rails by iron spikes driven through oval holes in the strips. The oval holes and tongue-and-groove cuts at the ends of the iron rails allowed for expansion and contraction of the metal. Metal plates were placed underneath the points where the iron rails were joined. Bloodgood noted that although the plates provided greater strength at those stress points, rail wear was faster at those reinforced places than elsewhere. He also observed that after the railroad was in use, the wrought iron rails became magnetic.[50] Some sources on early railroad history describe the resultant injury and death caused by the rail joints working loose, followed by the rails suddenly being pushed by the wheels upward through the floor of the carriages and

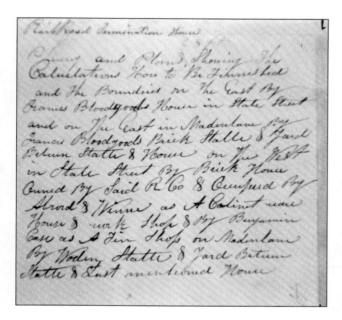

Above: Enlargement of site location description.

Right: Plan for railroad "termination" house on State Street in Albany. Courtesy of the Jervis Collection

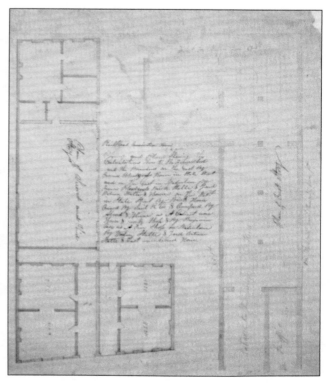

ripping along the floor as the car continued down the track. Such loose rails were called "snake heads."

By August 9, 1831, due to Jervis's expertise and exacting management of the laborers,[51] a single track of the projected double track line had been completed from the foot of the inclined plane in Schenectady to the junction of the Great Western Turnpike (Western Avenue) and Lydius Street (Madison Avenue) in Albany.[52] At that intersection, there was a "significant problem." Although the Great Western Turnpike Company had granted the railroad permission to cross its road, it was upon the condition that the railroad could carry no passengers east of the crossing. As a result, "construction ended a short distance to the east of [The Great Western Turnpike] and was not continued on to the Hudson River until the matter had been resolved in 1832."[53]

Under the terms of the agreement, the railroad was permitted to build a branch from the Lydius Street intersection along the north side of the turnpike to Capitol Square (State and Eagle streets).[54] On January 8, 1833, cars commenced running on the State Street branch, with each car drawn the two miles to the junction with Lydius Street (Madison Avenue) by a single horse. Locomotive power was used beginning at the Lydius Street intersection.[55]

In January 1832, the directors of the company reported to the legislature that the "amount actually paid and disbursed in the construction of the road was $483,215" and that an estimated "$156,693 would be required to complete it."[56] By the time of this expenditure report, the Mohawk and Hudson Railroad had been in operation for five months.

Once the railroad construction commenced, the work went ahead rapidly—requiring only a year to complete the laying of one track. Of course, additional time was needed to complete the line between its two terminating points. But with most of the track put down across the plain between the two cities, operations could begin.

IV: The First Trains

THE CROWD grew in size and impatience on the morning of September 24, 1831. The anxious on-lookers awaited the gala marking the official opening of the Mohawk and Hudson Railroad, and all wanted the memorable opportunity to ride the rails to Schenectady, even though it was the second "official" trip.

Although five new coaches were made available for the event, they could not accommodate the crowd. As it was, eighty passengers made the trip to Schenectady. Among those in the coaches were chief engineer Jervis and resident engineer Clark, who served as conductor for the trip. Also present were C. C. Cambreling, company president; New York's governor Enos Throop; several other prominent politicians; Stephen Van Rensselaer III; Erastus Corning; Simeon DeWitt Bloodgood; Edwin Croswell, editor of the Albany *Argus*; Thurlow Weed, editor of the *Evening Journal*, Jesse Buel, Jr. of the railroad's engineering department; and William B. Winne, described as the "ancient penny post."[1] David Matthew was the engineer and John Hampson the fireman.

The locomotive intended for the notable occasion was the Mohawk and Hudson's second engine, the Robert Fulton, larger and more powerful than its predecessor, the DeWitt Clinton. But mechanical problems precluded the use of the English engine and the DeWitt Clinton was brought up. Only three of the coaches could be drawn by the smaller locomotive, but the trip was made in forty-seven minutes. The other two coaches followed, pulled by horses, and took a half hour longer to make the journey.[2]

Once at Schenectady, Cambreling toasted the new enterprise: "The Buffalo Rail Road may we soon breakfast in Utica, dine at Rochester, and sup with our friends on Lake Erie."[3] Cambreling's optimistic, predictive wish was not entirely beyond belief when considered in light of the DeWitt Clinton's thirty-five-minute return trip to Albany—pulling all five cars.

As auspicious as this occasion must have been, it took place six weeks after the first "official" trip between the two cities. It was on August 9 that David Matthew stoked up the DeWitt Clinton for the initial formal run to Schenectady. The trip was described by an E. L. H. (possibly Mr. Hays, the High Constable, who was among those in the second car). He referred to conductor John T. Clark as the "Master of Transportation" and said that Clark, "after collecting the tickets which had been sold at the Hotels and other places for this excursion, mounted his seat at the back of the tender & blew his tinhorn for the signal to start."[4]

The event also was recorded in word and in silhouette by William H. Brown, a passenger on one

Silhouette by William H. Brown from his *First Locomotives*.

of the coaches pulled by the American-built locomotive. Brown described the train as including "some five or six passenger-coaches. . .of the old-fashioned stage-coach pattern." Three were unaltered from this design, but the rest were "surmounted with seats made of rough plank to accommodate the vast crowd of anxious expectants" who wanted to experience "this first ride on a railroad train drawn by a locomotive."[5] Brown's silhouette rendition of the engine, fuel car, and some of the coaches is pictured in his locomotive history. It has been frequently reproduced, although one of the facsimiles does not accurately capture either Brown's work or the occurrence, as the silhouette artist himself noted. The spurious illustration was the work of the Antique Publishing Company in Boston and was copyrighted in 1870, a year before Brown's book appeared. A ludicrous aspect of the Antique Publishing Company's version was the offer of a reward for copyright infringement that appeared on its print containing the erroneous account of the event.

Brown's description of the trip included incidents that were both problematic and humorous. Fortunately, Brown was an inside passenger, since "there were no coverings of awnings to protect the deck-passengers upon the tops of the cars from the sun, the smoke, and the sparks, and. . .the combustible nature of their garments, summer coats, straw hats, and umbrellas, soon became apparent."[6] In addition to being subjected to a showering inferno, the hapless riders also were in for other surprises. The train left the station with "a sudden jerk, that bounded the sitters from their places, to the great detriment of their high-top fashionable beaver [hats], from the close proximity to the roofs of the cars."

The passengers, having recovered from their unscheduled trips to the ceiling and undoubtedly to the car floors, were then treated to an exciting ride of "considerable velocity"——that is, until the train's arrival at a water station, which meant another "sudden jerk." While the locomotive was taking on water, American ingenuity solved the unplanned and discomforting dislocations. The links in the chain couplings between "the cars were stretched to their utmost tension" and a rail from a nearby fence "was placed between each pair of cars." The wooden rails were held in place by using "the packing-yarn for the cylinders, a bountiful supply being on hand (as the. . .brass-ring substitute had not then been invented)."[7] Except for frightening the horses attached to the numerous carriages and wagons that carried onlookers who flocked to witness the unbelievable

happening, thereby causing "innumerable capsizes and smash-ups. . .and the tumbling of the spectators in every direction[,]" the train arrived at the head of the Schenectady inclined plane without further event.[8]

Ten days after the adventuresome and auspicious excursion, the Mohawk and Hudson announced a regular schedule for the transportation of passengers between Albany and Schenectady. Trains would leave from Lydius Street in Albany at 6:30 A.M., 10 A.M., and 5 P.M. and from the head of the Schenectady plane at 4:30 A.M., 8 A.M., and 3 P.M. The trip would cost fifty cents.[9] In less than a week, traffic on the railroad had risen to three to four hundred passengers each day. It was predicted that the company's annual income would reach $140,000, and that would cause its stock to soar as high as 700 percent over its current trading price.[10] As it turned out, this speculation was widely over optimistic. Even so, the Mohawk and Hudson was moving ahead "full steam," remarkable for a railroad that had taken delivery on its first locomotive less than a month earlier.

The anticipation of the breath-taking and historic events of the summer and early fall of 1831 was heightened when the Albany *Gazette* proudly announced on July 29 the arrival of the railroad company's first engine by Hudson River tow boat from the West Point Foundry. At least the newspaper reporter sounded as though he was conversant with locomotive technology when he described it as "a beautiful engine" with "admirably constructed" wheels and its two cylinders "neatly and handsomely made." The reporter was confident that the power of the engine of such a machine "must be that of fifteen horses." Patriotically it was deemed "deserving of great praise" as a "specimen of the superiority of American workmanship." Certainly, "great credit" should go "to the agent Mr. Cambreling, for the rapid execution of this most admirable work."[11]

The genesis of the locomotive that was so regally welcomed took place on March 15, 1831, when a contract was negotiated between the West Point Foundry Association and the Mohawk and Hudson Rail Road Company. The former would deliver a locomotive engine for $3,200 and two twelve-horsepower high-pressure horizontal steam engines for $4,050. The specifications for the locomotive called for it to have a boiler and a pair of cylinders "of sufficient capacity force to propel Ten Tons on the Rail Road at the rate of Fifteen miles per hour on an elevation of one foot in two hundred and twenty five feet."[12] The locomotive design was based on a pre-

Novelty Iron Works, New York. Partly owned by Horatio Allen, the Works
was typical of those in the 1830s and 1840s that manufactured heavy iron products.
Author's collection

viously presented plan that called for the maximum weight of the engine not to exceed 6,200 pounds. The delivery date was set at no later than July 1, "in the city of New York." Subsequent agreements were signed for the delivery of sixty pairs of railroad wagon wheels with axles for $3,300, and a set of four wooden wheels complete with iron tires, axles, and eccentrics for the locomotive for $700.[13] William Kemble signed for the West Point Foundry and James Renwick for the Mohawk and Hudson. The railroad's chief engineer, John B. Jervis, was designated as inspector of the material to be delivered.

As described by David Matthew, its principal builder, the DeWitt Clinton had two inclined cylinders, each five and one-half inches in diameter with a stroke of sixteen inches. All four wheels were drivers, each measured four and one-half feet in diameter. The wheel spokes were turned wrought iron, and the hubs cast iron. The wooden wheels had wrought iron tires, or rims. There were inside cranks and outside connecting rods to connect all four wheels. The boiler was the tubular type with copper tubes each two and one-half inches in diameter and six feet long. It was fired by a drop furnace and the pumps worked vertically by bell crank. The engine was designed to burn anthracite coal and operate at thirty miles an hour pulling three to five cars on level

terrain.[14] Its three and one-half tons plus the weight of the 115 gallons of boiler water could be "very easily moved by a single hand" while it stood on the rails.[15]

The DeWitt Clinton was tested throughout July 1831 and its defects corrected. The water in the boiler surged so much that it flooded the cylinders. This was remedied by placing a high steam chamber on top of the boiler to allow for better expansion. The eduction pipes were not high enough in the chimney, and the chimney, or smokestack, was too large. All this resulted in a poor draft and was changed. Perhaps the most disappointing problem with the operation of the DeWitt Clinton was its failure to burn the coal for which it had been designed.[16]

It seemed logical that Jervis would intend the locomotive to burn anthracite coal. When the Delaware and Hudson's Stourbridge Lion was first fired during tests at the West Point Foundry in June 1829, hard coal from the Lackawaxen region of Pennsylvania was used. Both the Tom Thumb and the York, two Baltimore and Ohio engines used prior to the DeWitt Clinton, burned anthracite coal. Thomas Earle, a contemporary Jervis consulted, recommended the use of coal in his *Treatise on Rail-Roads*, and included descriptions of the geography of the Pennsylvania anthracite regions.

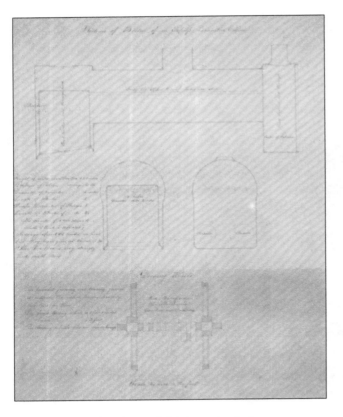

Plan of boiler and driving wheels for an
express (passenger) locomotive

But, when used in the DeWitt Clinton, the hard
coal packed in the engine's furnace to such an extent
that an air blast was necessary to fire the coal. When
the artificial blast was introduced, the heat was so
great that it melted the furnace grates and even the
nozzle of the pipe from the wind reservoir. The fuel
was changed to wood.[17]

On August 12, 1831, Maurice Wurts, one of the
founders of the Delaware and Hudson Canal Company, corresponded with Jervis on the problem of
burning coal in the Mohawk and Hudson's engine.
Wurts cautioned that there were "few persons that
succeed well in their first attempts" at the use of coal
to fire locomotives. He reported to Jervis that it was
"said that your draft is not good, and that the fire was
stirred too much, but as such occasions [sic] every
thing is said." Wurts then reflected that he had
"thought the last objection of little consequence the
first is made by a practical man and may be deserving
of your notice."[18] The Delaware and Hudson's founder may have been attempting to be helpful in his
advice. Certainly, he would have wanted the locomotive to burn coal successfully; it would have been
profitable for his coal company.

But Wurts might also have been trying to cover
up a problem with his company's product. By the
end of 1831, Jervis was apprised of another possible
cause for the failure of the DeWitt Clinton's coal-
burning experiment. James Renwick informed the
engineer in late December that he "had the misfor-
tune to try to burn Lackawaxen coal in my house this
season, and I can now understand why it did not
succeed the quality that company had sold this season
will not burn."[19] "That company," the Delaware and
Hudson, ironically was Jervis's former employer.

The DeWitt Clinton continued in use through
the end of 1831, when operations were suspended
until the following April. Winter weather affected
the running of locomotives. Extreme cold caused
wheels to slip, making it necessary to use horses to
pull the cars.[20] It took horse-drawn cars between
sixty-eight and seventy-five minutes to make the trip
to and from Schenectady. The locomotives did it in
thirty-eight to forty-six minutes.[21]

When traffic resumed in April 1832, the Clinton
was having problems, and $700 was paid to the West
Point Foundry for two pairs of wheels and eccentrics.
Apparently the defects of the locomotive involved
more than wheels and eccentrics, since it was still
inoperative in late April.[22] The water tubes in the
DeWitt Clinton leaked, and Jervis wrote to Adam
Hall, one of the engine's builders, to complain. The
chief engineer called Hall's attention to the superior
manner in which the tubes were fastened in the
Robert Fulton, the railroad company's English engine. Jervis lamented that he was "apprehensive we
shall not make her [DeWitt Clinton] worth much
after all." In disgust he added that the engine's operating cost was as much or more than horse power.
Jervis admonished Hall on the poor quality of workmanship demonstrated by the locomotive's faulty
performance and noted, sarcastically, "if the engine
goes well, with a good load, there is no doubt about
the beauty of the thing."[23]

Hall replied quickly and defensively that the
boiler tubes had been adequately tested. He believed
the problem resulted from a combination of an im-
proper water level in the boiler and the lack of an
experienced locomotive engineer.

Jervis's reaction is not known. The Clinton continued to malfunction, making it necessary to install
a new boiler before the end of 1832. Finally, after
apparently removing it from service in late 1833, the
company disposed of the engine in April 1835.[24]

The American-manufactured locomotive was
not the only engine used by the railroad in 1831.

42

Jervis recommended the purchase of an English engine in November 1830. He wanted one which would weigh between three and three and one-quarter tons, including boiler water, equally distributed on all four wheels, with sufficient power to pull its load at an average speed of twelve miles per hour. In addition, Jervis specified "the Top of the flue not to exceed 15 feet above the surface of the rail."[25] The chief engineer also indicated his preference as to the type of locomotive that should be ordered. He informed the corporate managers that the "attention of the English public is mostly occupied by the Engines on the plan of the Novelty and those on the plan of the Rocket." Jervis noted that the Novelty appeared "to be the favorite, although it has had only a very partial test. . .and I very much doubt if the expectations that have been raised will ever be realized by either the proprietors or the public."[26]

Having expressed his reservations about the Novelty, Jervis came out in favor of a machine similar to the Rocket. But he professed no knowledge of a locomotive made on the plan of the Rocket "of so small dimensions or weight as that proposed," which might therefore require making moulds or patterns, which could increase the total cost. Nonetheless, Jervis was adamant, since he regarded the importance of a light engine to be too "great to allow such difference in the expense to have any essential influence."[27] Yet, when the English locomotive was made, history was repeated. As had been the case with the Delaware and Hudson's Stourbridge Lion, the English machine turned out to be much heavier than Jervis's weight specifications.

The eagerly awaited product of the Robert Stephenson works in New Castle-on-Tyne arrived on August 27, 1831, two and one-half weeks after the initial public run of the DeWitt Clinton. Named the Robert Fulton, it was similar to the engines that Stephenson was building for the Liverpool and Manchester Railway. Bloodgood described it as "compact in appearance and [it] weighed 12,742 pounds, of which eight thousand seven hundred and forty-five rested on one pair of wheels. The frame is as long as that of the DeWitt Clinton [11 feet 6 inches] and is mounted on wooden wheels strongly bound with iron."[28] The locomotive's two cylinders, ten inches in diameter, had a stroke of fourteen inches and were "in the lower part of the chimney and are kept warm

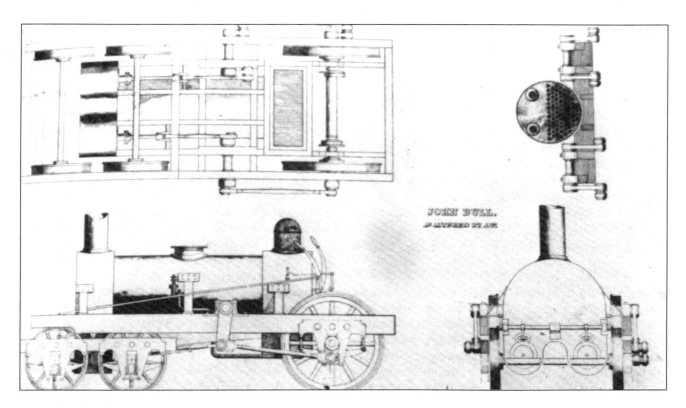

Drawing of the Robert Fulton as rebuilt in 1833 to a 4-2-0 design and renamed the John Bull.
From White's *The American Locomotive*

by the smoke and hot air."[29] It was the nearly four and one-half tons pressing on one pair of wheels that gave Jervis cause for concern, since the weight on a single wheel was two and one-half times greater than the heaviest load on a wheel of the Clinton.[30] The chief engineer was worried about the weight compressing the track's iron strip into the wooden rail, a problem that he faced with the Stourbridge Lion.

A detailed description of the construction and operation of the Robert Fulton was furnished to the Mohawk and Hudson Company by a Stephenson company clerk in July 1831. Apparently, it was accompanied by an illustration which, unfortunately, has not survived, although other drawings of the machine do exist. Construction details such as the placement of copper tubes in the boiler and their relationship to the fire at one end and to the bottom of the chimney (smokestack) at the other, are discussed. The bottom of the chimney was made large enough in order "to get the flame and current of heated air which goes through the tubes into a quiet state so as not to blow the ashes up the chimney." Next, the placement of the pistons, piston rods, and connecting rods was explained so that the transmission of power from the steam cylinders to all the wheels became clear. The engine was "set in motion by the man [engineer] turning the handle of the steam cock and then operating upon the starting handles," which were connected by a series of "levers" and "small rods" to the "slide valves of the engine." It was noted that in the "regular course of working, the engine moves the slide valves itself by means of the excentric [sic] and frames," and that only when the locomotive was to be started or stopped were the handles "called into action."[31]

Directions also were included for reversing the engine. This was done by means of an "apparatus" located "near the bottom of the fire place by the man [locomotive engineer] placing his foot upon a pedal near the fire door." The writer of the instructions cautioned that "this should be done as seldom as possible without first" shutting off the steam cock.[32]

While the personnel at the Stephenson works were confident that the English locomotive could easily pull twenty tons, they advised the Mohawk and Hudson that twelve tons would "be much better for it and [it] will last an adequately proportional time longer." The meaning of "adequately proportional" was not explained. In addition, it was noted that a small grade of one foot in 225 would "affect the working of the engine very little."[33]

Even though the Robert Fulton was a product of a company "then the best and most experienced manufacturers of locomotives in the world, [it] had to be materially altered before it was a practical success."[34] The alteration followed a design pioneered on the Mohawk and Hudson Railroad by John B. Jervis. It represented Jervis's major contribution to the development of railroad locomotives and would be incorporated in nearly all future engine designs. Jervis ordered his new, landmark machine from the same company that built the DeWitt Clinton, the West Point Foundry, headquartered in New York City.

The West Point Foundry's first locomotive built for the Mohawk and Hudson Railroad was less than satisfactory. Actually, the railroad company's engineer had indicated dissatisfaction with the foundry several months before the Clinton experienced problems in the spring of 1832. The previous December, correspondence was exchanged between Jervis and foundry superintendent William Kemble. Jervis expressed concern that a contract for rolling stock was altered to the advantage of the foundry. Evidently, Kemble changed an order for wheels and axles to include seats for the passenger cars. Jervis challenged Kemble's inclusion and asked "what right or where can there be the least propriety of your assuming to changefor seats that you now furnish . . ."[35] Jervis purposely did not order the seats manufactured by the company because they were not up to his standards. Other items, such as tools, also had been sent without being ordered. Jervis itemized the unordered materials, plus those for which he felt the company had overcharged, and deducted the cost from the foundry's bill.[36]

The objections Jervis had to the workmanship at the West Point Foundry and the lack of trust he had in its management did not prevent him from ordering his novel locomotive from the company. Perhaps it was in deference to the fact that both his friend James Renwick and Governeur Kemble, Mohawk and Hudson directors, also were on the board of the foundry.[37]

Articles of agreement were signed November 16, 1831, for the new machine to be built to Jervis's specifications. It was to be named Experiment, a fitting title because its design differed from those used on English railroads, which, of course, served as models for American locomotives. Actually, the brief instructions contained in the agreement do not suggest a difference from other contemporary locomotives. Curiously, they were reasonably specific in

The locomotive Experiment (also known as the Brother Jonathan) as rebuilt with wood-burning firebox.
From White's *The American Locomotive*

regard to many aspects of construction, except for that which was the most remarkable.

The wording specified that a seasoned white oak frame would support a round boiler containing copper flues to carry the heat from the rectangular furnace (five feet long, thirty-four inches wide, and made to burn anthracite). Attached to the "front end" of the boiler would be a "proper fixture. . .to receive a glass tube for a steam and water gauge so arranged as to admit of taking out a broken glass and conveniently substituting a new one." As a precaution, "three extra glasses properly prepared" were to be included.[38] Tie rods passing longitudinally through the boiler would be used to secure the boiler ends. A "good and convenient hand force pump, with copper pipes" was specified "to connect with the water tank on the Tender waggon." Also, the oil cups provided for lubrication were "to be constructed with a cotton-wick syphon as, in the [Mohawk and Hudson's] Stevenson [*sic*] engine."[39]

Cylinders nine inches in diameter with a stroke of sixteen inches would transmit power in the novel locomotive; each cylinder would be equipped with a "force pump and all necessary steam and water valves and pipes, eccentrics, rods, and other parts to make the working gear complete for the use intended."[40]

The "working wheels" or drive wheels would be made of cast and wrought iron of nearly the same design as those on the DeWitt Clinton. The one difference was that the wrought iron rims on the Experiment drive wheels were made with a flange, the "other wheels to have cast iron naves with wooden spokes and felloes and wrought-iron flanged tire or rim."[41] The Mohawk and Hudson agreed to pay $4,600 for the seven-ton machine, provided it was ready to ship from New York City on April 1. If not, the railroad company had the option to refuse delivery.[42]

The requirements for the "other wheels" were the only hint in the agreement that something might be different about this locomotive. Something was very different. Instead of the Experiment resting on four wheels fixed in position, the Jervis design substituted a four-wheeled truck in place of the two front wheels. The truck's purpose was to guide the rear driving wheels into curves on the railroad. David Matthew portrayed the moveable, or bogie, truck as having four wheels, each thirty-three inches in diameter. The "truck was placed under the front end of the boiler for support, attached by a strong pin, and worked upon friction-rollers so as easily to follow the curves of the road. . . ."[43] Matthew proudly and wondrously proclaimed that in testing the engine he "crossed the Mohawk and Hudson Railroad from plane to plane, fourteen miles, in thirteen minutes, making one stop for water." The locomotive engineer incredulously asserted that on a section of straight, level track he "made one mile in forty-five seconds [eighty miles per hour] by the watch." He announced that the Experiment was the "fastest and steadiest engine I have ever run or seen, and she worked with the greatest ease."[44] This was the "first bogie engine or truck . . . ever built in this country or any other."[45]

Although understandably pleased with his accomplishment, Jervis never claimed to have invented the moveable truck. He was the first, however, to successfully apply the principal to a locomotive. Undoubtedly the well-read Jervis was aware that William Chapman, an English inventor, patented a "bogie" truck in 1812. Meant for use on rail wagons, the wheels of Chapman's truck "moved around the rail or circumference of the curve as the vehicle above it took the chord of the arc."[46] Jervis certainly also knew of Tredgold's writings on English railroads, since a copy of the book with Jervis's personal notations was in the engineer's private library. Tredgold described eight-wheeled carriages with two moveable trucks. His description includes the statement, "If one frame with its four wheels be removed, and an axis with two wheels applied in its place, the carriage would have 6 wheels, and it would be easy to adjust the load so that the pressure on each pair of wheels would be equal."[47] Essentially, this is what Jervis did in designing the Experiment. Jervis's contribution in this regard should not be underrated.

While it is true that Jervis did not patent his moveable truck engine, he frequently and emphatically defended his claim to being solely responsible for its introduction. Much of this was prompted by the contention that others had developed a truck locomotive earlier than Jervis did. Most notable of the contenders was Horatio Allen, who desinged the locomotive South Carolina. Allen's contract to construct the Charleston and Hamburg line allowed him to be absent during the summer in order to avoid the unhealthy season in the South. During the summers of 1830 and 1831, Allen journeyed to the Albany area in order to spend his leave time with Jervis and to observe the work on the Mohawk and Hudson.

Both Jervis and Allen worked on a solution to the problem of developing an engine that could negotiate curves with ease and yet run at high speed, since the emphasis at the time was on passenger trade. Because merchants and other potential railroad investors were aware of the low cost per ton-mile to ship goods by water, they continued to assume that trade in heavy freight could not be taken from water transport. Jervis and Allen each had a "lively impression of the failure of the Stourbridge Lion and were specially intent on devining [sic] a relief for the rails [distributing the weight] by some method of increasing the number of wheels."[48]

Jervis noted that the English method of solving the problem was to place the weight on more wheels, but to keep all the wheels on the same frame. Both he and Allen regarded this as impractical for use on curved track. Jervis's main concern was not whether his plan would work, but whether it would perform safely on curves at high speed. He discussed the plan with Allen, who apparently liked it. The two men had an "extremely cordial" relationship and "interchanged the various views [they] entertained in a most frank and unreserved manner."[49]

Eventually, though, the discussions between Jervis and Allen led to a divergence of views concerning the truck engine. Allen became committed to a plan for a double-truck engine on eight wheels, which was simply to connect two frames to a single boiler and firebox. He felt it necessary to take this approach in order to maintain an adequate number of drivers. However, Jervis disliked its complexity and saw problems arising from the "working of machinery on two frames that must be constantly varying their parallelism."[50]

Allen's South Carolina was built in 1831 and put into service the following year. Jervis wrote in his autobiography that had the South Carolina been successful, he would have rejoiced at Allen's achievement. But, as Jervis pointed out in a letter to the editor of the *Railroad Gazette*, his plan was a success and Allen's a failure. In the forty years since the introduction of the two plans, "I do not know that Mr. Allen's locomotive is seen on any railway. Mine may be seen on 50,000 miles of railway," Jervis wrote.[51]

In reflecting on his innovation, Jervis admitted that he lacked complete confidence in the reliability of the truck. It was Allen who, impressed with the idea, assured him that it would work safely. In fact Allen was the "only engineer of any considerable experience who favored [Jervis's] views."[52]

In any case, as Jervis admitted, credit for the invention of the truck principle could go to neither him nor Allen. "All we are entitled to," according to Jervis, "is our respective plans for adopting this principle . . . to passenger speed."[53] This point was reiterated by Jervis at the conclusion of the section on the Mohawk and Hudson in his autobiography. "The truck itself was not a new idea with me," he emphasized, since "it had in principle been used, but was generally supposed to be impracticable for high speed."[54]

The Jervis claim to the forward moveable truck engine has been accepted by several historians who have concentrated on the development of American railroad technology. William H. Brown credited Jervis with originating the truck plan for locomotives. Robert Thurston, in a history of steam engines published seven years after Brown's book, also recognized Jervis as responsible for the new type engine. Thurston wrote that in 1832, "the first locomotive

was built of what is now distinctively known as the American type engine with a truck or bogie under the forward end of the boiler." It was built at the West Point Foundry "from plans furnished by John B. Jervis."[55]

More recently, Brian Hollingsworth, an English railroad expert, described Jervis as "one of the great benefactors of mankind. . .who in 1832 introduced the pivoted leading truck or bogie" in locomotives. Contemporary verification of Jervis's pioneer effort also can be found in John White's history of American locomotives. According to White, "the six-wheel engine or 'Jervis type' enjoyed a brief but intense popularity in the United States. It performed well in mixed service and was our first national type, a distinctive American locomotive." White noted that the "great years for the 4-2-0 [wheel arrangement] were between 1835 and 1842 when it was built almost to the exclusion of any other wheel arrangement." White explained that the boiler and valve gears were a direct copy of the standard Stephenson design, but the running gear was a radical departure from the type used on British engines.[56]

This new "distinctive American locomotive" design resulted from Jervis's observation that the rigid frame of English locomotives was not satisfactory for American tracks. Locomotive builders were quick to adopt the Jervis-designed 4-2-0. One of the most

Horatio Allen's design for a locomotive that could negotiate curves at increasingly higher speeds.
From Brown's *First Locomotives*

notable, Matthias Baldwin, visited the Mohawk and Hudson Railroad, was favorably impressed with the Jervis truck engines, and built his next locomotive, the E. L. Miller, on the Jervis plan. White pointed out that in accord with common practice concerning locomotive reforms, Jervis failed to patent his design and it was "freely given over to the industry."[57]

Jervis was understandably proud of the Experiment, as mechanically it was a great success. Unfortunately, the Experiment experienced the same problem that initially existed in the DeWitt Clinton

Although anthracite coal was intended as fuel, the five-foot long firebox was a failure, and in 1833 it was replaced with a wood-burning firebox.[58]

The Mohawk and Hudson Railroad truly was a pioneer in the development and use of the locomotives. Its earlier 0-4-0 English locomotive was rebuilt on the new plan, and the new wheel arrangement also was adopted by the Saratoga and Schenectady Railroad, as well as by those railroads that would soon be constructed between Schenectady and Buffalo.

V: Another Railroad

BEFORE the end of 1831, when the Mohawk and Hudson Railroad had been in operation for only a few months, some of the proprietors began to turn their attention to what amounted to a continuation of the line in the form of a second railroad company. It was still deemed impossible to compete with the Erie Canal, even if the state legislature had been willing to grant a charter to compete with the state's canal, as it did two years later for the Utica and Schenectady Railroad. As a result, attention was directed northward from Schenectady to the village of Saratoga Springs.

A favorite watering spot, the spa was a destination for those who desired to "take the cure" or to simply vacation in that early resort. It seemed logical to the railroad entrepreneurs to extend the Mohawk and Hudson's track to Saratoga, only a little more than twenty miles from the Mohawk River terminus of the Mohawk and Hudson, passing through Ballston Spa about half way.

While construction continued on the Mohawk and Hudson, plans also went ahead to build the line to the spas. By February 16, 1831, the act to incorporate the Saratoga and Schenectady Railroad Company passed the state legislature. The act gave the new company approval to build a single- or double-track railroad from Schenectady to Saratoga, a distance of approximately twenty-two miles. Two years were

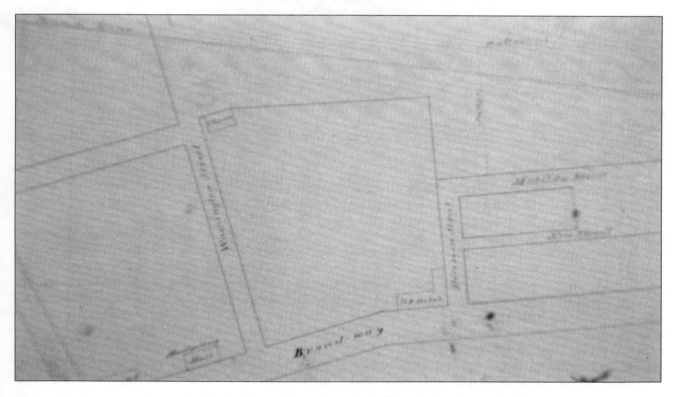

Detail of the route of the Saratoga and Schenectady through the village of Saratoga Springs showing Broadway south of the rail line. The U.S. Hotel is in the lower right center. Courtesy of the Jervis Collection

allotted for the start of construction, which by law had to be completed within five years. Capitalization was set at $150,000 initially, with the option to increase to a maximum of $300,000 if necessary. In addition to the three communities already mentioned, Albany and New York City were added to the places at which the stock could be subscribed.[1]

After allowing for the usual acquisition of the right-of-way, protection of the landowners, and other privileges that would accrue to the company in order to construct the line, the legislature again protected its own property. The act specifically forbade the construction of the railway across the Erie Canal "without the written authority of the canal commissioners." But the commissioners were allowed to grant permission if evidence was presented that demonstrated it was "indispensably necessary to the construction of said railroad or way, and that it. . .shall not in any degree obstruct the transportation" on the Erie Canal.[2]

Churchill C. Cambreling was elected first president of the new railroad and John B. Jervis was chosen as its principal engineer. According to the company by-laws, the secretary had to reside in New York City. This rule might have been instituted in deference to the fact that, as was the case with the Mohawk and Hudson, a majority of the directors lived in the great metropolis. Many members of the Saratoga and Schenectady board were simultaneously directors of the Mohawk and Hudson.[3]

In addition to specifying terms for company officers, duties of the collectors and agents, and the matter of compensation, the by-laws also contained a prohibition clause of sorts—"no spirituous liquors" could be "sold by any agent, tenant, or other person," on company property.[4] This was a curious inclusion, given the considerable and widespread consumption of alcohol at the time. But it also may have been a sign of the general tenor of temperance reform underway during the 1830s.

Churchill C. Cambreling
Library of Congress

On March 21, 1831, engineer Jervis informed the Saratoga and Schenectady directors that he had completed preliminary surveys of two potential routes and that both appeared satisfactory. He estimated either route would cost a little over $10,000 per mile, for a total of $221,267.62. But, Jervis cautioned the directors, "if it should be thought important to travel at a greater velocity than 10 miles per hour it may be effected by adopting a carriage proportionably lighter or by constructing a stronger road."[5] Jervis favored the stronger road, even though it meant an additional cost of more than $1,000 per mile. Jervis also recommended a track gauge of 4 feet 9 inches in order to allow the rolling stock to have the same wheel dimensions as those of the Mohawk and Hudson.[6]

Another aspect of Jervis's "stronger road" that was somewhat novel to railroad construction at the time was proposed by his subordinate engineer, William C. Young. Young suggested "the use of cross-ties in lieu of stone blocks and foundations, which formerly sustained the sleeper to which the strap-rail was spiked."[7] Actually, Jervis had used cross ties to a limited extent on the Mohawk and Hudson. Undoubtedly, Young was aware of this when he pushed for their use on the Saratoga and Schenectady. Finally, all but three miles of the road rested on cross ties.

As usual, Jervis carefully described their use. According to the engineer, in this type of construction a longitudinal timber was laid to support the wood rail. Then, "on this timber the cross sleepers are laid at three feet from centre to centre; the cross sills have a notch (or gain) cut to receive the longitudinal sill, and also to receive the rail timber, which is secured to it by wedges."[8] In keeping with the common practice, the timber rail was capped with an iron strip or plate. Jervis observed that building a railroad with cross ties was less than half as expenseive as constructing one on a stone foundation. This was a

Above: English lithograph of the Utica and Schenectady Railroad at Little Falls. The locomotive in this 1839 print is the English type that would not have been used on New York railroads at that time. Wood rails are supported by cross ties of the type pioneered on the Mohawk and Hudson and the Saratoga and Schenectady.
Author's collection

Right: Kayerderrosas Creek bridge.
Courtesy of the Jervis Collection

Below: Route map of the Saratoga and Schenectady Railroad.
Courtesy of the Jervis Collection

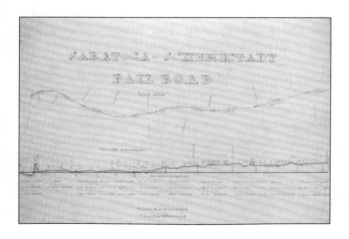

major advantage, especially in America, where timber was plentiful but capital was not.

Jervis also commented on the "apprehension [that this type of construction] would suffer much from frost." In defense, he observed that "the experience of the past winter, however, has not confirmed the fears" and "if the road is well and uniformly drained, the frost affects it but little. . .and when the ground is settled in the spring, this kind of road is very readily adjusted."[9] Apparently this was true, since it was reported in the spring of 1833 that the Saratoga and Schenectady experienced no serious damage from frost during the previous winter, therefore the "annual repairs will be unimportant."[10]

Jervis predicted that a wooden cross-tie foundation would not be as hard on the railway carriages as a stone foundation, but for the "same reason," traction would not be as good.[11] The reference was to the elasticity of a wooden tie rail base over that of a stone base.

The Saratoga and Schenectady Railroad opened for business on July 12, 1832. Its length from the Mohawk River bridge at Schenectady to Saratoga was 21.4 miles. The single-track road was constructed over level land and undulating terrain with grades not "exceeding 16 feet in a mile, or at a rate of 1 foot in 330."[12] The total building cost was $217,201.22, which included carriage houses, stables, and two other dwellings. This amounted to $10,149 per mile, just slightly over Jervis's initial estimate. Land acquisition was not included in the construction costs.[13]

Due to the expense needed to bridge the Mohawk River with a structure capable of bearing the weight of an entire train, the company arranged to lease a highway bridge, even though the bridge could handle only one car at a time pulled by horses. Despite this bottleneck, the trip from Albany to Saratoga could be accomplished in three and one-half hours.[14]

The somewhat undulating nature of the topography between Schenectady and Saratoga contrasted with the nearly level plain between Schenectady and Albany. Since the six-wheeled truck engine already proved the worth of its superior design on the Mohawk and Hudson, the chief engineer of the Saratoga and Schenectady knew what was required for that railroad. A Jervis-type 4-2-0 locomotive was ordered, but not from the West Point Foundry. The order was placed with the English firm of G. Stephenson and Company.

It was warm and sunny outside the Saratoga and Schenectady's New York City office on July 18, 1833, when the company engineer described the new engine. The glorious weather seemed to herald the dawn of a new era in locomotive technology. Now, even the vaunted English manufacturers would start production of the American design. The transfer of technology that began in England in the late 1820s had gone full circle.

It was not that six-wheeled engines had never been produced in England; they had been made there several years prior to 1833. The goal was to distribute the weight so the locomotives would be less injurious to the track. But the major problem with six wheels under a single frame was that the design did not accomplish what the builders desired—because of the unevenness of the tracks, the load of the engine tended to bear unevenly on the wheels. Added to this dilemma was the fact that the early six-wheeled engines did not negotiate curves as well as four-wheeled engines did, since the latter locomotives could be geared much shorter. The English abandoned the use of six-wheeled engines and were not manufacturing them at the time the Saratoga and Schenectady order arrived.[15]

The new locomotive was named Davy Crockett and, as Jervis designed it similar to his Experiment, it was mounted on two separate frames. The smaller frame would be supported by four wheels, each thirty-two inches in diameter. One end of the bigger frame was supported by the two larger drive wheels. The other end "rested on friction rollers in the centre of the first frame, to which it is secured by a strong centre pin."[16] This arrangement allowed the small wheels under the front of the locomotive to negotiate a curve with ease. They guided the working or driving wheels around curves in a manner that eliminated much of the usual vibration and the "machinery of the engine [was] not affected by the curve motion of the carriage."[17]

When the eagerly awaited machine arrived, it was set up in the Mohawk and Hudson shop and tested under the supervision of chief mechanic Asa Whitney. Whitney had been hired at a salary of $800 per year plus all work-related traveling expenses.[18] The engine proved to be all that was expected. It rounded curves "without any more appearance of labor than a well geared common carriage," moved "with almost as smooth and steady a motion as a stationary engine," and traveled "over the road in an elegant and graceful style."[19]

When it went into operation on the run between Schenectady and Saratoga, the Davy Crockett was heralded as "one of the most complete locomotives which have been invented." This sounded as though the engine was one of the great wonders of the world. Perhaps it was to those who saw it, since it was known to have the power to pull three baggage wagons and eight carriages with 160 to 180 passengers at speeds of at least twenty miles per hour.[20]

In any case, the new locomotive was "capable of drawing 15 tons at the rate of 17 miles an hour, and even more, with about 5 bushels of coke, which will cost perhaps 10 or 12 shillings." In other words, it could "do the work of 50 horses, which are an expense of $50 a day, for the comparatively trifling sum of $15 a day . . ."[21] As proof of the engine's capabilities, on July 2 the Davy Crockett left Schenectady pulling a train of freight wagons, "overtaking a train of passenger cars at Ballston, which it took up in addition [this train was pulled by horses] and with these arrived at Saratoga in one hour and forty minutes, stoppages included."[22] It then returned to Schenectady and on its second trip to the spa on the same day shaved ten minutes from its previous time. This was done with only thirty pounds of steam, against such obstacles as a heavy thunderstorm and muddy rails. One of the passengers seemed overcome when he exclaimed that "dur-

ing some part of the way, the speed was at least thirty miles per hour!"[23]

Later, Jervis commented on speed and its relationship to the single pair of drive wheels. He recognized that the use of the forward, four-wheeled swivel truck limited the adhesion or traction of the locomotive to its rear drive wheels only. But, he pointed out, adhesion of only one pair of wheels "is hardly of any importance when high speed is wanted."[24]

The Saratoga and Schenectady's English-made Davy Crockett proved so superior to the fixed, four-wheeled locomotives that a decision was quickly made to rebuild the Mohawk and Hudson's Robert Fulton, also built in England. The job was done in the Mohawk and Hudson's shops under the able supervision of Asa Whitney. But the alteration proved unusually difficult. The Robert Fulton was a Stephenson Sampson class engine, with its cylinders inside the main frame. This necessitated the use of bell cranks to connect the cylinders to the rear drive wheels. Once the Robert Fulton was rebuilt, the American steamboat pioneer's name was dropped in favor of the English moniker, John Bull.[25] Thus

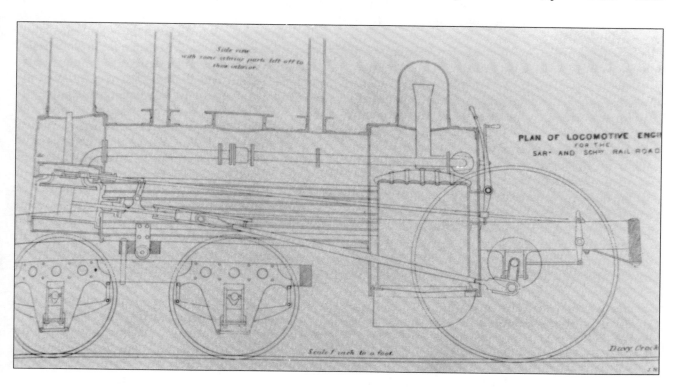

Saratoga and Schenectady Railroad locomotive Davy Crockett built by
Robert Stephenson & Co. in 1833 to Jervis's design.
From White's *The American Locomotive*

 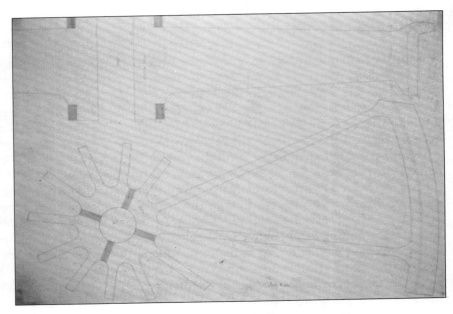

Left: Plan for improved railroad wheel by John B. Jervis. From *American Railroad Journal*, July 20, 1833
Right: Plan of original Jervis rail wagon wheel. Courtesy of the Jervis Collection

altered, the John Bull performed as well as the Davy Crockett, and "the ease and smoothness of her motion, over that she had when on four wheels, [was] very striking."[26]

In the short time since their opening, New York's two capital district railways had introduced new methods of track construction and pioneered novel locomotive design, and in doing so paved the way for the march of rails from the Hudson River to the Great Lakes. Virtually all of the innovation was the work of their chief engineer. Although he accomplished much, Jervis was not satisfied or willing to rest on his laurels. His next contribution to railroads was the development of an improved wheel for railroad wagons. The redesigned wheel was introduced on the Saratoga and Schenectady.

The earliest coaches used on the Mohawk and Hudson were, for all intents and purposes, stagecoach bodies mounted on four wheels adapted to run on railroad track. One source described the initial coaches as products of the works of James Goold of Albany.[27] In business since 1813, Goold was one of the largest stagecoach manufacturers in the state.[28] The first six vehicles were furnished by Goold at a cost of $310 each.[29] But another person, a participant in the "Initial Trip of the First Railway Train in America to carry passengers," referred to the "cars or coaches" as "stage coach bodies furnished by Thorpe & Sprague coachbuilders & [the coaches] were placed

on trucks and were hung on leather straps similar to the stage coaches of that period."[30]

Coaches, or passenger wagons as they soon were called, also were obtained from the West Point Foundry. Jervis designed the wheels for these wagons and later improved his original design.[31] The new design was made public in an illustrated article in the *American Railroad Journal* published in the summer of 1833. The first requisites for these new three-foot diameter wheels were defined as lightness combined with a "good chill for hardening the face of the rim and flange" to achieve adequate strength. The engineer explained that due to the width necessary for the track of the rim, it was not practical to manufacture the rim wider and heavier in the best form to assure the greatest strength to resist the pressures in the direction to which it was exposed. To compensate for this, and the lateral strain acting upon the wheel while in routine use, the spokes were made very wide in proportion to their mass. Although this tended to lessen the spokes' ability to resist vertical strain, Jervis's design compensated for this by the use of reinforcing ribs on the sides of the spokes. Since the entire wheel was cast iron, as opposed to the more expensive wood and wrought iron wheels, the importance of perfect casting was stressed.[32]

Jervis admitted that his original design for the wheels used on the Mohawk and Hudson was prone to failure. Those wheels each supported between three-quarters and seven-eighths of a ton. They were run at an average speed of fourteen miles per hour and, during the first year of use, experienced roughly a 25 percent rate of failure. The new wheels with the reinforcing ribs, or "feathers" as Jervis called them, weighed 275 pounds each, or twenty pounds more than the original design. Evidently, the added "feathers" proved their worth, since in a year's usage, not a single passenger carriage wheel broke. Although the average running speed was fifteen miles per hour, the wheels "have often been run under that load [passenger carriage] at a speed of twenty miles, and in some instances at twenty-five miles per hour." Jervis felt the one-year test results proved the wheels safe and that the two railroads had no need to turn to the more costly wood and wrought iron wheels.[33] The wheels

were another example of the innovation that occurred in the building and operation of the Mohawk and Hudson and Saratoga and Schenectady railroads.

Even before Jervis improved the carriage wheels, new and larger passenger carriages were being designed which ultimately would be supported by the improved wheels. The larger coaches were built in Schenectady and were "of a square form, fifteen feet long, with the separate compartments, and will contain 18 persons with ease."[34] The coaches, with their "soft cushions and panelled walls," were heralded as a major improvement, since the passengers would have more room and, perhaps more important, would be "protected from the smoke and coals of the engine."[35]

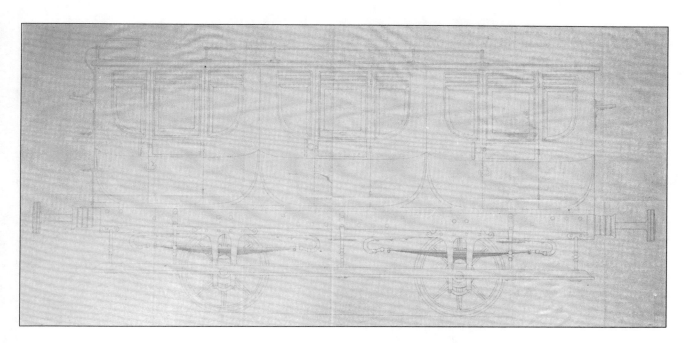

Drawing on linen of an early four-wheeled railroad coach.
Courtesy of the Jervis Collection

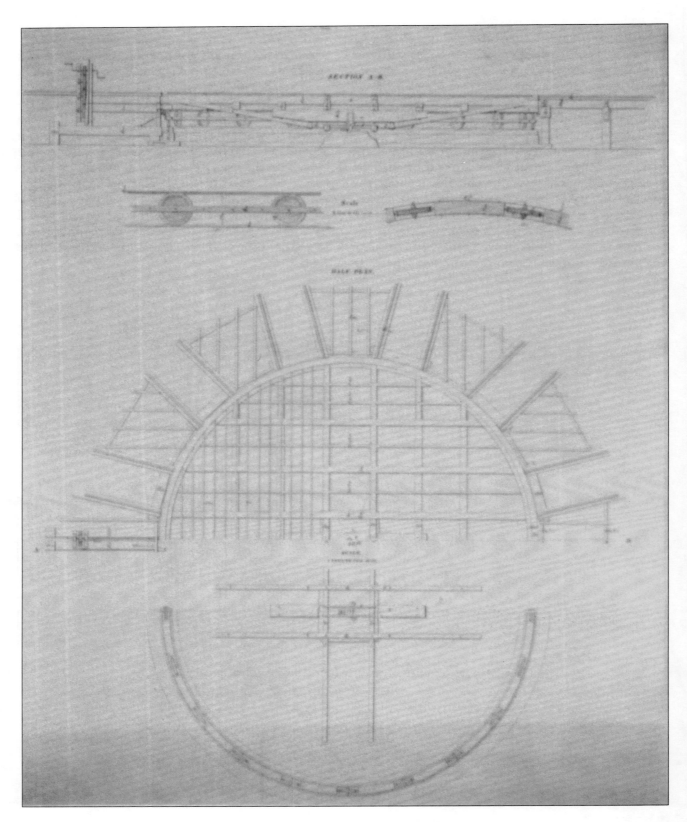

Turntable—Mohawk and Hudson Railroad.
Courtesy of the Jervis Collection

VI: Running Railroads

On April 3, 1833, John B. Jervis submitted his resignation as engineer and superintendent of the Mohawk and Hudson Railroad. Asa Whitney was appointed to succeed him as superintendent and agent, at an annual salary of $1,500 plus the use of a house.[1] The change in job title indicated the evolution that had occurred with the end of the initial construction stage.

Jervis returned to building waterways, and more than a decade passed before he built his next railroad, the Hudson River line. Two months before he resigned, he submitted a thirty-nine page report on operations and projects for the Mohawk and Hudson. The report revealed the condition of the railroad in early 1833 and the outlook for the future.

Jervis opened his report by informing the company president and directors that the second track extending from the junction of the main line and branch line near the Western Turnpike in Albany to the head of the inclined plane in Schenectady was nearly completed. The clay embankments, particularly the one at the Albany inclined plane, had stopped shifting, and Jervis felt it would require no additional expense to stabilize them. But the horse path between the rails would need attention. The path initially was constructed with broken stone which turned out to be unsatisfactory—the stone continued to be dug up by the horses' hooves, which not only destroyed the path but injured the horses as well. Jervis recommended the use of slate gravel, even though it would cost more in upkeep.[2]

Next, Jervis addressed the 12.3 miles of fence (3,949 rods) that would be required to secure the line, particularly from animals. At between five and twelve cents per rod, the total cost estimate was $3,800.[3] This would be money wisely spent, he reasoned, as animals could be no small problem for railroads. An example of the damage that animals could cause occurred two years after the Jervis report on the neighboring Saratoga and Schenectady line. In its edition of July 27, 1835, the *American Railroad Journal* carried a report of an accident on the Saratoga

and Schenectady involving a cow. Apparently the locomotive was not equipped with a "cowcatcher," and when it struck a cow standing on the track ran over the animal, resulting in the engine leaving the track. The consequence was considerable damage to the locomotive, injury to several passengers, and, of course, death to the cow.[4] Cowcatchers at the front of locomotives helped to prevent animals from rolling underneath the engine when hit and causing a derailment.

The estimates Jervis presented for buildings in his report provide a contemporary description of the size and cost of railroad structures. Jervis advised the construction of a building eighty-five feet long and thirty-four feet wide, which would house fifteen of the largest carriages (passenger cars). The cost, including "turning platforms" (turntables) and side roads, would be $1,100. The engineer also felt the company should build more houses for workers near the head of the Schenectady inclined plane. He noted that several of the railroad workers lived in Schenectady, a mile from the line. Since this was "particularly inconvenient for starting the early trains," it would be advantageous "in having the men, whether engaged in the Shops or in Transportation, reside near their work."[5] Jervis recommended the construction of two duplex houses at $800 each and one single-family residence at $500. Of course, the $2,100 investment could be recouped by rent paid by the workers.[6]

The report also included detailed estimates and accompanying recommendations relative to the differences in cost between horse power and steam power, both in terms of the stationary engines at the top of the inclined planes and the locomotives. Comparing the traffic on the Albany plane with that on the Schenectady plane, it was found that thirty-two carriages, or twelve more per day, were used on the Albany inclined plane. The three teams in use on the Schenectady plane cost six dollars each day in upkeep and drivers' wages. This was equal to the amount of oil and fuel plus the fifty-cent daily wage of the operator of the stationary steam engine. The greater traffic on the Albany plane produced a fifty-cent daily advantage in favor of the engine.

Although the cost of operating steam engines on the inclined planes was not significantly less than the cost of horse power, Jervis favored the use of steam. As usual, his position was supported with pertinent statistics. He confidently advised the company officers that "there cannot be the shadow of a doubt" that steam power should be used in overcoming the elevations at both ends of the railroad. Those who do not "critically examine" the differences fail to consider "that every 20 feet elevation overcome by horse power is equivalent to one mile on a level road."[7] In other words, it required double the horse power to ascend twenty feet in a mile than to pull the same load on a level.

Jervis also compared the use of horses and steam locomotives on the level between the two inclined planes. He calculated that ten teams (twenty horses) would be needed on a daily basis. Each team, including the wages for the drivers and grooms and the cost of shoes and harnesses, would cost a minimum of $1.87 each day. Then, estimates of the amount needed for breakage of the connecting shafts were made. Jervis found this difficult to determine, but noted that horses that have the "requisite courage for Rail Way travelling are often difficult to manage." He believed that their propensity to break shafts would be greater, causing him to raise his calculated daily cost of each team to $2.[8] This worked out to two-thirds of a cent per mile based on a team's ability to pull carriages with an average occupancy of twenty passengers fifteen miles in a day.

A locomotive could move 420 passengers in a day from the head of the Schenectady plane to the junction at Albany, the extent to which engines were permitted to travel. At that time, the Mohawk and Hudson's agreement with the Great Western Turnpike Company permitting the railroad to cross the turnpike did not allow passengers to be carried across

A page from the Erie Canal field book of Thaddeus R. Brooks, Little Falls, June 4, 1838.
New York State Archives

the toll road to the railroad's eastern terminal at Gansevoort Street.[9] The daily operating expense of locomotives including repairs was put at $17, or one-third cent per mile——half the cost of horse power. Jervis cautioned that his calculations were based on an "active" business. An increase in operating cost "of from 50 to 100 per cent" could be expected as a result of "an irregular and light amount of work.[10]

To carry the passengers and freight, Jervis advised the purchase of fourteen additional carriages and wagons at a total cost of $3,875. The three passenger coaches made to be pulled by either horses or locomotive and to accommodate sixteen inside passengers in all seasons would be $800 each. The six "passenger and freight wagons" were calculated at $112.50 each, and the five wood wagons, exclusive of wheels (which would be furnished from the railroad's stock), could be purchased for $160 per wagon.[11] The wood cars had to be sturdy enough to bear the weight of both hard and soft wood. Jervis estimated the weight of a cord of mixed hardwood at 4,000 pounds "half seasoned," and pine at an average of 2,500 pounds. This wood was for market and not for locomotive fuel, although the locomotives burned wood, also; attempts to use anthracite (hard) coal had been unsuccessful and trials had not been conducted using bituminous (soft) coal.[12]

By agreement with the turnpike company, a branch rail road north of the toll road to the center of Albany was permitted. The railroad company decided to build along State Street from its intersection with the Western Turnpike (Western Avenue) to Capital Square at Eagle Street. The branch was completed by the end of 1832 and went into operation January 8, 1833. But unequal settling resulted from the tracks being laid so soon after grading. Sand was brought by rail from the sandy plain through which the line passed and was used to level the land under the rails. This was the least expensive solution to the problem.[13]

A much more serious difficulty was affecting the pavement between the rails. The "common country waggons" were of a width that permitted their wheels to track inside the Mohawk and Hudson rails. The teamsters had "a strong propensity" to steer wagons between the railway rails, "which brings all the action of their wheels on one point and that where the pavement comes against the rail timber." The result was "a rut formed which exposes the work of the road to injury."[14] Jervis's solution was to recommend a course of "oak scantling 4 by 5 inches covered with a plate of rail iron coming up as near the top of the rail as to admit the free operation of the flange of the [rail car] wheel."[15] The result was a track in the street similar to that later used by street cars.

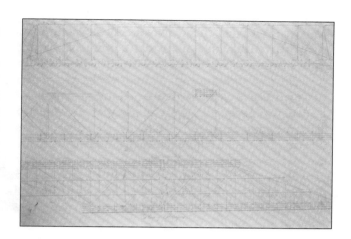

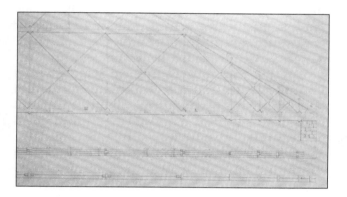

Right, above: Mohawk and Hudson/Saratoga and Schenectady railroad bridge drawings. Courtesy of the Jervis Collection

Right: Plan for a large bridge, possibly over the Mohawk River at Schenectady—Saratoga and Schenectady Railroad. Courtesy of the Jervis Collection

Below: Plan for the Morning Kill bridge—Saratoga and Schenectady Railroad. Courtesy of the Jervis Collection

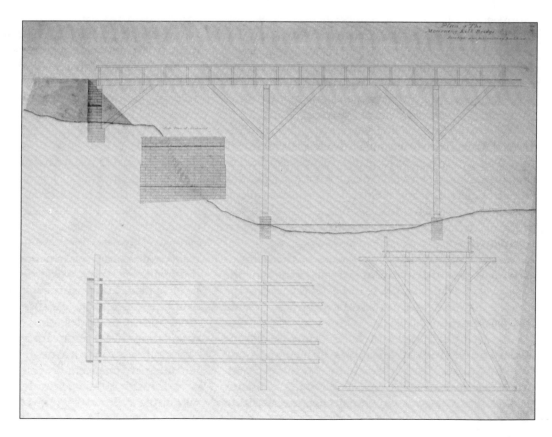

Before leaving the Mohawk and Hudson, Jervis used his friendship with canal commissioner and future governor William Bouck to get permission for the Mohawk and Hudson to build two bridges across the Erie Canal at Schenectady. Rapid assent from Bouck was given for the company to construct a "common road bridge" and a railroad bridge. Jervis informed the board of directors that he also asked for the widening of the canal across from the company property at Schenectady. Presumably, this was to provide a basin for docking canal boats waiting for the transfer of passengers or freight between the railroad and canal.[16]

The articles of freight carried by the railroad included the mail. Apparently the Mohawk and Hudson was offered the opportunity to transport mail regularly carried by a company that ran a stage between Albany and Schenectady. Perhaps the proposition offered by Thorpe and Sprague was an indication of the extent to which the railroad had affected their business. Thorpe and Sprague proposed relinquishing the mail business if the railroad would deliver mail to them free of charge. Jervis noted that an additional railroad carriage would have to leave Albany at 9 P.M., and that one would have to be in readiness in Schenectady at all times "to take the mails when they arrive from the West." Although "some additional expense will be incurred in accepting this arrangement," Jervis also frugally noted that "an additional number of passengers will be secured." After all, he reminded the railroad directors, this extra mail business should be profitable, since "we now carry the Mails that come at our regular times of starting in either direction," anyway.[17]

Of course, railroading was in its infancy in the United States and the passenger trade even relatively new to the railroads of England. Procedures such as the collection of fares that we now take for granted were not clear or standardized then. For example, it was the practice of collectors on the Mohawk and Hudson to collect the fares after the passengers boarded the train. This method was used out of necessity, since the passengers were in the habit of arriving at the office (station) just before the time the train was scheduled to leave. If the collector took the time to take the fares at the office, the train would not start on time.

It should be noted that by the time he left the Mohawk and Hudson, Jervis was both engineer and superintendent. In other words, he was charged with managing operations as well as directing construction. In his manager role, Jervis called the attention of the directors to the wasteful and inefficient method of fare collection. It apparently resulted in overlooking some passengers and making mistakes in making change with others. Jervis noted "that about $70 has been received at Albany during the past summer from passengers who had not been called on and who voluntarily offered their fare at the end of the route." The ever-vigilant Jervis suggested a change that would facilitate a more efficient method of fare collection: His solution was to require that tickets be purchased before the carriages left the starting point. To make this more expeditious, Jervis suggested the collector be assisted by a clerk.[18]

The remainder of Jervis's report was taken up with route plans and cost estimates for extending the branch line to the docks in Albany. He confined his survey to two routes, one along State Street, and the other by way of Hudson Street. Although Hudson Street had the advantage of a more graduate slope, the State Street route was shorter and, perhaps most important, much less costly. To run the line via Hudson Street would cost more than five times the $5,374 needed to build along State Street.[19]

Almost buried in the builder's parting statement was a prediction for the future of the railroad. When opened for business, the Mohawk and Hudson's outlet to the west was the Erie Canal. It was built to complement the canal by providing a shorter route for passengers between Albany and Schenectady. Initially, freight was not considered a profitable commodity. Conventional wisdom, as expressed by the Buffalo *Journal* in 1831, the year the Mohawk and Hudson commenced operations, agreed that railroads could not successfully compete with canals in carrying goods.[20] Jervis disagreed with this assumption.

By April 1833, the Utica and Schenectady Railroad was incorporated. Jervis had knowledge of the organizing efforts for this road because he referred to it in his report. He reasoned that if a railroad "extended from Schenectady to Utica there would be an extensive business in those lighter freights that demand expedition."[21] Then, counter to the belief that shipment on water was immune to competition, Jervis added, "the transportation on the Rail Road could be effected for less than the price paid on the canal and in much less time." Jervis probably was speculating that freight cars would be hauled by the two railroads on a through basis; unloading and reloading at Schenectady would not take place. Support for this idea is found in his statement that without a railroad to Utica, "the freight business would not extend much beyond the counties of Schenectady and Saratoga." In saying this, he ruled out the use of the Erie Canal, since "the inconvenience of transshipment would operate against the Rail Road on all freight."[22]

Jervis's willingness to challenge waterways with railways was reiterated in the mid-1840s, when he prepared extensive calculations to demonstrate that a railroad adjacent to the east bank of the Hudson River could successfully compete with the vaunted water route. The Hudson River Railroad did so, and in 1869 was joined with the New York Central to become the mighty system that dominated trade between New York City and Chicago.

Two months after filing his insightful report, Jervis resigned from his position as engineer and superintendent. Asa Whitney was a good choice to follow the highly competent Jervis, as was noted in a resolution by the board of directors commending him in June 1834. Eleven months later, Whitney was more tangibly recognized with a $1,000 salary increase. Then, in May 1836, Whitney resigned to pursue other business interests. Peter L. Parsons, company freight agent, was appointed to replace Whitney. Parsons, who lasted only until the end of March 1837, was briefly succeeded by civil engineer W. H. Talcott until June, when Whitney returned. For the next two and one-half years, Whitney vigorously managed the company's affairs.[23]

Asa Whitney left the railroad company for a second time at the end of October 1839. Apparently, the company directors chose to "reward" his exemplary service by suggesting that his pay be reduced by nearly 50 percent as a cost-saving measure. The man who brought the Mohawk and Hudson through the worst years of the Depression of 1837 was replaced by John Costigan. Costigan's service as superintendent lasted more than three and one-half years before he was suddenly terminated in June 1843. It is not clear why Costigan was fired. Among his succes-

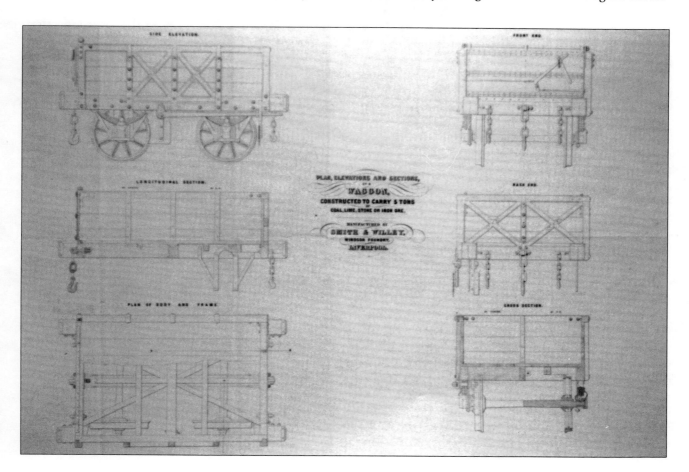

Drawing of a coal wagon (English).
Courtesy of the Jervis Collection

sors was John T. Clark, a resident engineer who worked for Jervis while the road was under construction. Later, in 1853, Clark was elected to the post of state engineer of New York.[24]

Beginning in 1836, all who managed the Mohawk and Hudson had to cope with the western railway connection. In that year, on the first of August, the Utica and Schenectady opened for business. Until then, the only other railroad doing business with the Mohawk and Hudson was the Saratoga and Schenectady. From the opening of the latter, these two early railroads were "systematized" to the degree that their limited track mileage and traffic allowed. This meant that by 1833 the two trains leaving Albany to take passengers to their ultimate destination of Saratoga Springs had to be coordinated at Schenectady with the trains leaving that city for the spa.[25] After 1836, this relatively uncomplicated procedure changed radically. The debut of the Utica and Schenectady was followed in 1839 by the Syracuse and Utica. Four years later, four additional railroads opened rail traffic to Buffalo and Lake Erie. This meant that New York's first railroad undoubtedly would have to plan for the scheduling of connecting trains, the transfer of passengers and baggage, the division of rates, and the exchange of equipment. The relative simplicity of its early operations gave way to increasing complexity.

An example of the growing complexity can be found in an early account of freight carried on the Utica and Schenectady Railroad. During its first eight years of operation, the Utica and Schenectady was forbidden by law from carrying freight. The New York Legislature protected its Erie Canal by eliminating potential competition from a railroad that closely paralleled the canal for the entire seventy-eight miles between Utica and Schenectady. In 1844, the legislature relented and allowed freight on the Utica and Schenectady, but only during those months that the Erie Canal was closed. Even then, on all freight carried by the railroad, the Utica and Schenectady "shall pay the same tolls per mile as would have been paid on [the freight] had it been transported on the Erie Canal."[26] This handicap notwithstanding, the shipment of merchandise commenced immediately. In 1844, the Erie Canal ended its navigation season on November 26;[27] the Utica and Schenectady started moving freight on November 27.

The list of merchandise transported on the railroad for late 1844 and early 1845 reads like a general store inventory. Because of the manner in which the

ledger was set up, not only can the account be used as a reference for goods carried on the Utica and Schenectady, but also for freight transportation on the Mohawk and Hudson and on the Syracuse and Utica, as well. In addition, the listing isolated those items which emanated from the Mohawk Valley region, the area that was immediately west of Schenectady and closest to the Mohawk and Hudson. Of course, as one of the two easternmost rail links in the growing chain of roads between Albany and Buffalo (the other was the Schenectady and Troy Railroad, opened in 1842), the Mohawk and Hudson funneled goods and people to and from the Hudson River. The importance of the information contained in the record is such that it is reproduced on the facing page.[28]

The 1826 act of incorporation for the Mohawk and Hudson did not restrict its freight transportation business other than to prohibit the railroad from charging more to move merchandise than the combined amount of tolls and charges for the same goods on the Erie Canal. But, without the rail connection to the west, the difference between the mid-1840s and a decade earlier was striking. From December 14, 1834, two days after the seasonal closing of the canal, through the end of January 1835, the tally for goods shipped from Schenectady to Albany was:[29]

Item	Dec. 1834	Jan. 1835
Dry goods, in bales & boxes	20	0
Shoe pegs, bags	9	0
Hats, boxes	0	27
Mittens, "	0	1
Books, "	0	0
Congress water, "	1	10
Tools, "	0	1
Flaxseed, bags	0	12
Printed sheets, etc., bundles	0	81
Leather, sides, rolls & boxes	2	204
Hair, sacks	0	1
Piano-fortes, boxes	0	1
Flour, barrels	99	82
Ashes, "	0	4
Provisions, bbls. & hogsheads	58	0
Butter, firkins	0	2
Liquors, casks, pipes, & bbls.	54	54
Luggage & Furniture, in lots	1	2
Hides, lbs.	1,600	0
Axel-Arms, "	886	0
Staves	6	0
Kettles, copper	22	0
Wood, cords	8	22
Boards, pieces	0	9,750
Lumber, pounds	3,200	16,000
Tierces, content unknown	1	0
Barrels, empty	4	8

Facing page: Annual account of property passing eastward and left at Albany. Utica and Schenectady Railroad November 27–December 31, 1844; January 1845

ITEM	Rec'd from Utica & Syr. RR		Shipped East of Utica Difference In Amount		Left at Albany	
	1844	1845	1844	1845	1844	1845
Fur, lbs.	16,848	34,894	(1,181)	1,511	15,667	36,405
Ashes, bbls.	18	20	63	68	81	88
Pork, '	2	2	125	33	127	35
Beef, '	126	16	481	226	607	242
Cheese, lbs.	15,389	15,231	68,484	147,859	83,873	163,090
Butter, '	48,655	70,587	245,979	29,581	294,634	100,168
Lard, '	400	629	2,758	447	3,158	1,076
Wool, '	19,682	47,700	(1,563)	(7,106)	18,119	40,594
Pork, '	34,588	112,948	129,093	100,441	163,681	213,389
Flour, bbls.	438	278	1,069	450	1,507	728
Other Grain, bu.	0	745	748	0	748	745
Bran & Ship Stuff, bu.	0	1,050	992	0	992	1,050
Peas & Beans, bu.	16	77	180	298	196	375
Dried Fruit, lbs.	1,000	5,933	19,001	(2,304)	20,001	3,629
Tobacco, lbs.	0	170	695	50	695	220
Clover & Grass Seed, '	7,048	124,821	5,154	622	12,202	125,443
Domestic Spirits, gals.	4,360	15,480	30,120	42,440	34,480	57,920
Leather, lbs.	2,494	9,925	124,253	32,784	126,747	42,709
Furniture, lbs.	15,847	2,110	6,979	4,691	22,826	6,801
Paper, '	1,875	3,886	15,955	(162)	17,830	3,724
Iron Ware, '	2,169	1,223	11,239	2,431	13,408	3,654
Domestic Woolens, '	36,771	19,869	52,725	37,802	89,496	57,671
Domestic Cottons, '	15,608	15,725	112,336	70,854	127,944	86,579
Poultry, '	43,714	41,165	122,862	20,504	66,576	61,669
Hops, '	0	0	8,541	0	8,541	0
Sundries, '	83,454	47,144	58,900	26,893	142,354	74,037
Barley, bu.	0	0	87	0	87	0
Potatoes, bu.	0	0	3	0	3	0
Boards & Scantling, ft.	0	0	10,980	0	10,980	0

The aggregate weight amount and revenue was, for December: 131,104 pounds at 3.125 cents per 100 pounds, for a total of $40.97. For January it was 425,408 pounds at 3.125 cents per 100 pounds, totalling $132.94. In other words, the Mohawk and Hudson Railroad shipped just over 278.25 tons of goods in the last month of 1834 and first month of 1835 for which it received $173.91. Taking only the merchandise for which the items were listed in pounds that the railroad carried in December 1844 and January 1845, the total for the mid-1840s was almost four times greater than the amount for the mid-1830s.

The effect of the western railroad connection on the passenger trade is more difficult to determine. Since its opening, the Mohawk and Hudson received passengers at Schenectady from the Erie Canal, and at Albany from the Hudson River. Beginning in 1836, the Utica and Schenectady brought people to the Mohawk River terminus of the Mohawk and Hudson. From Schenectady, the Mohawk and Hudson took them to Albany. The opening of the Utica and Schenectady notwithstanding, the number of people who rode both ways on the Mohawk and Hudson in 1836 actually declined from the previous year. Passengers in 1835 numbered 172,790 which, incidentally, was the railroad's biggest passenger year during its first ten years of operation. The following year's total dropped to 159,737 passengers. It is true that passenger use increased by 350 in August 1836, the month following the opening of the Utica and Schenectady. Yet, for the remainder of the year, the number of people carried by the Mohawk and Hudson was 1,662 fewer than the number of passengers carried August through December 1835.

The only apparent factor that might have influenced a reduction in riders after August 26, 1836, was a first-class fare increase from 62.5 cents per one-way trip to 75 cents. But, the adverse impact of the increase would have been minimal, since residents of Albany and Schenectady were exempted from the increase if they purchased round-trip tickets.[30] Also, the decline in passengers for 1836 was much greater prior to August. When compared with the first seven months of 1835, the passenger loss for 1836 was 11,391 between January 1 and July 31. Given the statistics that show the decline in riders was nearly seven times greater prior to the opening of the Utica and Schenectady on August 1, 1836, than for the months after it opened, a logical conclusion would be that the western rail link for the Mohawk and Hudson saved it from even greater passenger losses.

Whatever the cause may have been for the passenger decline in 1836, the dramatic loss in the passenger trade in 1837 that continued in 1838 could be explained by the onset of a depression in 1837. The severe national economic downturn lasted throughout the remainder of the decade. In 1837, only 138,203 people rode the Mohawk and Hudson. The following year the number of riders rose to an unimpressive 143,607. Although in 1839 ridership rebounded to a robust 167,206 people, perhaps a sign that the depression had not run its course was the drop in passengers to 147,722 in 1840.[31]

Of course, the erratic passenger business had its corresponding impact on the railroad's net operating cost. In 1835, $66,171 was needed to run the railroad. By the following year, the decline in income from fares caused the operating cost to rise to $78,850, and in 1838 the amount increased again to $83,099. Not until 1840 did cost of running the Mohawk and Hudson drop back to the low sixty thousands.[32]

A similar dip in passenger business was felt by the Saratoga and Schenectady as a result of the hard times. Peak "pleasure" season traffic from Albany via Schenectady fell from 3,777 riders in 1836 to 2,453 in 1837, then rebounded some to 3,090 for June, July, and August of 1838.[33] Receipts followed the trend with $41,018 received from passengers in 1836, $25,596 the following year, and a less than notable $32,118 generated in 1839. With average annual expenses running about $21,400, the net profit was at times less than spectacular.[34]

Operating expenses included salaries of officers and agents, workers' wages, repairs to the road, coaches, engines, wagons, horse feed, and other incidentals. By 1839, the Mohawk and Hudson Railroad was divided into eleven categories for operational purposes. They were: Albany Branch Termination; Schenectady Termination; Engine and Plane West End; Machine Shop; Locomotive Steam Power; Wood Shop; Blacksmith Shop; Engine and Plane East End; Store House East End; Store House West End; and Maintenance of Way. In June, ninety-five regular workers were employed by the railroad, exclusive of company officers.[35]

There were fourteen employees at the Albany branch termination. Wages ranged from $25 to $30 a month, with the most common at $26 for drivers. Only H. C. Southwick, the collector, was salaried at a relatively princely $800 per year. At the Schenectady termination there were only half the number of workers as at Albany, and the collector there earned a little over half as much as Southwick. But there were twice as many employed at the west end plane as at the east end, which had the services of only four men. The daily wage of the east end engineman, the highest paid of the crew there, was 12 shillings (12½¢ per shilling); his counterpart at the west end earned 16 shillings per day. The firemen and drivers at the planes received $26 to $28 monthly. There were four employees each in the wood shop and blacksmith shop. Those in the wood shop repaired coaches and wagons for an average of 12 shillings daily. The blacksmith received 16 shillings per diem and his helpers only 7 shillings for their daily work. The nine men whose duty it was to maintain the right-of-way were listed as carpenters, with a superintendent receiving 18 shillings daily. He also supervised several day laborers along the line. The superintendent in the Machine Shop made $800 yearly to manage the shop and its five workers.[36]

Excepting various collectors, superintendents and freight agents, those ten persons listed under Locomotive Steam Power were generally the best paid. The three enginemen received 18½ shillings daily, their firemen made 9½ shillings each day, the brakemen, $28 per month, and the ticket collectors $35 monthly. But as well paid as those in locomotive steam power were, they did not match the income of the agents and tallymen in the store houses. Although most of the twenty-six people working in the two store houses (warehouses) were laborers and clerks who made $25 or $26 a month, the two freight agents and four tallymen definitely were in the railroad's upper-income bracket—each freight agent was salaried at $1,000 annually. Only Asa Whitney, general superintendent with an annual salary of $2,500, was paid more that the freight agents. One of the tallymen at the east end storehouse made $900 for the operating season, and the others received between $43.75 and $50 monthly.[37]

One other employee of the Mohawk and Hudson appearing on the ledger was Jacob Anthony. His job was described as that of "processing passengers over [rail]Road from S[team] Boats on the H[udson] River," for which he was paid $30 each month.[38]

The list of persons employed by the Mohawk and Hudson in 1839 provides a useful "snapshot" of the railroad's divisional organization, job descriptions, and wages typical of an ante-bellum American railroad. It demonstrates a rudimentary system development on a relatively short line. Additional insight into operations, requisites, and costs for an early American railway can be found in the company's "General Affairs Journal" for 1839-1843, inclusive.

This is particularly helpful in regard to insight into locomotive repair costs, fuel and horse power expenses, locomotive and carriage purchase prices, and other incidental expenses and income.

For example, in 1839, the railroad company listed four locomotives among its inventory: Mohawk, Hudson, John Bull, and Brother Jonathan. The Brother Jonathan was Jervis's original Experiment renamed. The seven-ton locomotive cost $4,600 when purchased from the West Point Foundry in 1832.[39] Of course, it was the first 4-2-0 steam locomotive. The John Bull was the redesignated Robert Fulton. It came from Robert Stephenson and Son in Newcastle at a cost of $4,900. Delivered in 1831, the six and one-quarter ton engine was rebuilt as a 4-2-0 following the success of the Experiment.[40] Apparently both the Mohawk and Hudson also were the work of the Stephenson shop. Both were 4-2-0 engines purchased in 1834 or after. They had forty-eight-inch drivers with ten-inch by fourteen-inch cylinders.[41]

Judging by the total engine repair costs for 1839, the English machines required more expensive maintenance than did the American locomotive. The Mohawk was the most costly to upkeep, at $904.93 for the year. This was followed by the Hudson at $622.32, and the John Bull at $534.46. The Brother Jonathan required only $391.02 in repairs for 1839.[42] The Company Journal does not record the extent to which each engine was used, nor does it detail the type of repairs made to each machine.

Between the end of June and the last day of October 1839, it cost the company $4,370.82 to fuel its locomotives. By comparison, the cost to feed the company horses was $4,736.69. The total expended for "locomotive steam power" for the following year was $3,748. During the same period, the cost for the "Engine and Power" at the western inclined plane was $3,124, and the same for the eastern plane was $1,562.[43] Also, at the end of the 1830s, carriages accommodating twelve passengers inside and six outside were purchased by the Mohawk and Hudson at $450 each, while freight wagons cost the railroad between $300 and $390 each.[44]

In addition to the income generated by passenger and freight transportation, the railroad also received payment from the Post Office Department for carrying the mail. In 1839 alone, this averaged nearly $1,250 per quarter. Another income entry that curiously appeared on the company's books for 1839 was thirty-seven cents received by the wood shop "for boards for a child's coffin."[45] Apparently the railroad's public service went beyond merely transportation.

At the end of 1840, the Mohawk and Hudson Railroad Company marked the culmination of ten years of operation. During its first decade, the railroad had expanded its business, added to its inventory of locomotives and carriages and everything necessary to operate them, coordinated its connections with two other railroads, and survived the disastrous economic downturn that hit in 1837. Even though the Mohawk and Hudson rebounded from the hard times that extended into the early 1840s, other events impacted the line during its second decade in business.

Almost prophetically, one of those changes was suggested by chance as early as the end of 1840. A solicitation arrived at the company offices from George R. McLaughlin of New York City. McLaughlin announced himself as the "inventor and proprietor of a machine designed to clear snow and ice from Rail Road tracks." He imaginatively called the device a "Snow-Plough" and pronounced it adept at removing the "one great obstacle to the running of locomotives and trains in winter." The device would "greatly facilitate the operation of cleaning the tracks, which now either lay idle for a considerable part of the year, or are rendered available only after great delay, trouble, and expense." After making reference to an important testimonial to the working of his "plough," the inventor assured that prompt attention would be given to an order if the railroad thought "that such an invention would be an object to your company."[46] It was noteworthy that the letter was addressed to the "President of the Albany and Schenectady Rail Road Company," not to the chief executive of the Mohawk and Hudson.

The corporate history of the Mohawk and Hudson was about to be altered in the 1840s, but the development of its railroad "cousin," the Saratoga and Schenectady, already had undergone a profound change. In 1832, some Troy businessmen organized the Rensselaer and Saratoga Railroad in order to capture control of the Saratoga passenger business from its nearby Albany rival. The new railroad was opened from Waterford to Ballston Spa on August 19, 1835, then extended across the Hudson from Waterford into Troy the following spring. The Rensselaer and Saratoga's proprietors and people in Troy began to buy Saratoga and Schenectady stock with the goal of capturing control of the older line. By late 1835, they were on the verge of succeeding. Correspondence between an officer in the Bank of Troy and General John E. Wool, one of his stockholders stationed in Charleston, South Carolina, reveals the extent to which the takeover of the railroad had been secured.

According to the correspondent, the bank president was "now in New York completing the arrangements in relation to the purchase of the Saratoga and Schenectady Railroad—a majority of which is owned by the Trojans." Bringing the railroad under the complete control of people in Troy would "secure a permanent arrangement for our cars [those of the Rensselaer and Saratoga] to Saratoga instead of Ballston Spa." He then added, "this troubles the Albanians some,"[47] no doubt because ownership of the Saratoga and Schenectady had to a large extent shifted from entrepreneurs in New York City, a place that complemented business in Albany, to a competing community across the Hudson River. Yet the Saratoga and Schenectady takeover by the Troy-based railroad did not occur in its entirety until 1851.

Detail of the plan for the viaduct across Washinton Street and Gordon Creek, Ballston Spa. Courtesy of the Jervis Collection

VII: Competition and Cooperation

THE UNITED STATES entered the 1840s still recovering from its first severe economic downturn. What started as a panic in 1837 soon degenerated into a depression, the impact of which was exacerbated by the extent to which portions of the nation had become industrialized.

New York State was in the forefront of the Industrial Revolution in America, and the depression, therefore, was hardfelt in the state. One after another, the state's numerous banks suspended specie payment. This meant that they were no longer able to redeem the paper money they had issued against their gold or silver reserves. Typically, the hard money deposits in the financial institutions were only a fraction of the value of the paper they had in circulation. As the bad times worsened, people began to draw on their bank deposits and redeem the paper money they held, thereby reducing reserves in the banks along with the banks' ability to cover outstanding paper. The resulting devaluation of paper money added to the downward economic spiral.

It is worth noting that at that time, even the federal government did not have the mechanisms in place to cushion the economy. Although the State of New York did have a bank Safety Fund to assist banks in trouble, the fund was soon depleted by the magnitude of the depression.

Naturally, the economic woes were not confined to banks, but spread to industry and business as well. That the Mohawk and Hudson survived the depression as well as it did could serve as a testimony to its management, in particular Asa Whitney, and to the continued population expansion in the country. Also a help was the aid the railroad received from the City of Albany, without which the Mohawk and Hudson would have been hard pressed to survive to mid-century.

National expansion, which was beneficial to the railroad business, continued apace. But a somewhat different twist was added by 1846, when the United States embarked on its first conflict with a foreign nation for the purpose of the addition of territory.

To be sure, wars had been fought with several Native American nations, resulting in national expansion. But the war against Mexico ended in a huge chunk of real estate coming under United States ownership. The addition of Texas was confirmed, and California and the entire Southwest became part of the land settlement obtained from the Mexican Republic.

Prior to the outbreak of the war in 1846, the United States finalized its hold on the Oregon Territory (mostly the present states of Oregon and Washington) as a result of a treaty with England. The territory's fertile land, coupled with the gold rush in California, drew more settlers west. This quickened the pace of frontier expansion that had continued actively since the beginning of the century.

Another component that drove internal expansion in the decade of the 1840s was the beginning of large-scale European immigration to America. Arriving from Germany, Ireland, the rest of the British Isles, and Scandinavia in ever increasing numbers, the newcomers poured into the eastern port cities. Two of the principal reception centers were New York City and Boston. The new arrivals that ventured westward from these ports tended to funnel through New York's Mohawk River valley, either via the Erie Canal or the railroads. At the beginning of the 1840s, the railroads between Albany and Buffalo were still unconnected, independent companies, but this would change out of necessity soon after the beginning of the succeeding decade.

The onset of the '40s found New York's canal-building boom continuing from its initial boost generated by the opening and huge success of the Erie in 1825, but at a slower pace. The recently organized Whig Party that in 1838 successfully edged the Democrats out of their long tenure in the governorship surrendered the chief executive's chair back to the Democrat Party in 1842. Actually, the Democrats had begun their drive to recapture control of the state by retaking control of the state legislature in 1841. At that time, the party's radical wing succeeded in passing a law that temporarily halted work

Pre-Civil War railroad passenger car showing wooden bench seats inside.
Smithsonian Institution of American History

on the Erie enlargement and some lateral canals until the state debt could be reduced through taxation. This was but a brief building respite; by 1844, conservative Democrats resumed canal work.

Both conservative Democrats and Whigs tended to agree that state government should continue aid for internal improvements. This largely meant public funds for canals, but also, to a much lesser degree, for railroads. Public support for railroads also took the form of aid from municipalities for the lines that served them, such as was the case with the Mohawk and Hudson. Backing from the City of Albany was crucial for the survival of that road in the 1840s.

Although public funds did go to railway corporations in the first half of the nineteenth century, the amount was minimal in comparison to the money poured into New York State waterway construction. In part, this was due to the perceived competition between the state's railroads and canals. The relatively small amount of public support for railroads also might have been attributed to the lingering suspicion that corporations were monopolies that worked against the concept of equal economic rights or opportunities then idealized by so many people. Public money should not be spent on private enterprise, or so it went. On the other hand, the state continued to be in the canal business. Tax dollars went into the several ditches that would connect many parts of the state with the Erie. Most state citizens generally agreed that this is how it should have been, since canal traffic on the mighty Erie continued on a steady upward climb, and so did the revenue from tolls. At least this was the case with the heavy freight business, even if passenger trade began to be siphoned off by the railroads. The railroads had speed on their side, although their fares, averaging about three cents a mile,[1] still could not match the two cents or less per mile charged by the canal packets.[2]

The cities between Albany and Buffalo, some of which owed their birth to the Erie Canal, continued their growth and development, fed by the persistent westward migration. In 1840, Albany had 33,721 people, Schenectady 6,784, Utica 12,782, Rome 5,680, Syracuse 11,013, Rochester 20,191, and Buffalo 18,213. By 1850 the numbers had jumped considerably, and by then Albany numbered 50,763, Schenectady 8,921, Utica 17,565, Rome 7,918, Syracuse 22,271, Rochester 36,403, and Buffalo 42,261.[3] Of course, by the 1840s, not only did New York's renowned waterway continue to serve these cities, but so did railroad lines, the Mohawk and Hudson among them.

Although the Mohawk and Hudson was the first of the roads linking the Hudson River and Lake Erie, competition from of other railroads soon materialized. In 1836, the Schenectady and Troy Railroad was chartered. (Troy is located to the north of Albany on the east bank of the Hudson River and is actually on a more direct line east of Schenectady than is Albany. The distance from Troy to Schenectady is only about five miles greater than from Albany to Schenectady.) The impending competition from another railroad triggered a reaction from "an Albanian" inquiring as to the effect of the new line "upon the interests of" Albany.[4] The letter warns the Mohawk and Hudson president of the expected consequences and offers advice as to how to cope with the challenge.

The correspondent alerted the railroad company president that a road connecting Troy and Schenectady would divert "so much of the business as to freight and passengers" from the Mohawk and Hudson as "to be the prejudice of this city" and "seriously effect [sic] our public houses, our labourers, and our whole sale dealers."[5] He then shifted attention to the dividends paid by the Mohawk and Hudson, and with grandiloquence claimed that in order to sustain the present dividend the company charged "upon passengers twenty per cent more than any other rail road in the world & fifty per cent more than most rail roads." Those who have stock in the Mohawk and Hudson, he wrote, "can not look calmly upon the establishment of a rival road, nor willingly submit to have their now very moderate dividend seriously reduced."[6] The dividend referred to in 1840 was three dollars per share, which totalled $30,000.[7] The letter writer admonished the company president that in the future, "you will be compelled to struggle to retain what you now enjoy and in the end the question may be submitted to your board whether the interests of the stockholder does not require the abandonment of your road."[8]

But the president and company officials need not have despaired, since the author of the correspon-dence had the solution to the Mohawk and Hudson's obvious problems: First, the inclined planes at both ends of the road had to be removed. After that, it was suggested that the railroad "unite with the Troy road at a point about half way between Albany and Troy."

The inclines needed to be removed, so went the argument, because as a result of the "present inclined planes and expensive horse power," the writer did "not hesitate to assert that the Troy road will be able to compete so successfully as to prevent your company from ever declaring a dividend after it [the Schenectady and Troy Railroad] shall go into operation."[9] By uniting with the Troy road, the writer claimed that the Mohawk and Hudson could save on "motive power," because the "power which you now use would be sufficient for both parties" and ownership of "one half of the road between Albany and Troy" would yield an income while reducing maintenance costs. The total annual savings was projected at $26,226.[10]

Although such dire happenings were forecast and "humble aid" offered to help correct the situation, apparently the dreadful events did not take place, at least not as a result of the opening of the Schenectady and Troy in 1842. During the remainder of the 1840s, the Mohawk and Hudson's business did not decline to the level of corporate extinction, nor did it combine with its new competitor.

But significant changes for the railroad between Albany and Schenectady did occur before the end of the decade. Principal among them was the removal of the awkward, expensive to operate, and increasingly complained about inclined planes. An act of the legislature, passed April 16, 1838, paved the way for the relocation of the planes, beginning with the one in Schenectady. The legislation authorized the railroad to construct new track as necessary, "so as to enable them advantageously to use and operate said road without the aid of stationary power."[11] Once this act passed, however, the question was no longer a legal one, but one of finance. Given the year in which the legislation was passed, finding money proved to be a difficult task.

The Panic of 1837 reduced the company's income and tended to dry up other sources of support. Of the two anchor communities of the road, Albany, with its much larger population and business community, seemed the best bet as a place to raise money. But the general shortage of capital and the Albany citizens' pledge of $1 million to finance the opening of a railroad route to Boston eliminated the Hudson River city as a source of funding at that time.

So, early in 1839, the Mohawk and Hudson directors turned to the state legislature. They requested a $250,000 loan of state credit to improve the railroad as permitted by the Act of 1838. The company's plea fell on deaf ears and the lawmakers refused to grant the subsidy.[12]

Failure to obtain funding for the removal of the planes led the company directors to resolve on June 15, 1840, to extend the line in Albany from its termination at Gansevoort Street north to Ferry Street at Broadway. The extension would bring the rails closer to the Hudson River, near the site of the Mohawk and Hudson's lower State Street extension it had abandoned in 1835. The track to Ferry Street was completed in September, 1841.[13]

costs and the purchase of iron rails.[15] The final cost to circumvent the Schenectady incline totalled nearly $92,000.[16] The new route, circling from Hamburg Street westerly around to the Schenectady station, opened in 1843.[17]

While work was underway on the new route to get around the western plane, the Albany Common Council turned its attention to the inclined plane in the city. On July 11, 1843, the council decided to borrow and lend to the Mohawk and Hudson Railroad "a sum not exceeding One hundred and twenty-five thousand Dollars" for a maximum of twenty-five years at 5 percent annual interest, payable semi-annually. The loan was to finance construction of "a new double track branch Road to some central point in

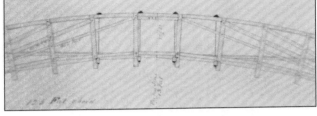
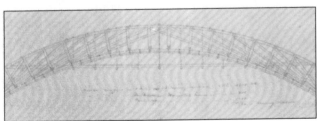
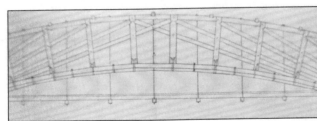

Railroad bridge plans with details—Saratoga and Schenectady.
Courtesy of the Jervis Collection

By then, the Mohawk and Hudson directors had again turned their attention to the removal of the inclined planes, energized by the threat of competition resulting from the impending completion of the Schenectady and Troy Railroad. A committee was appointed and empowered to borrow in order to pay the cost of eliminating the Schenectady plane. An issue of 7 percent bonds was authorized to cover the loan.[14] This action by Mohawk and Hudson brought a reaction from the City of Albany the following year. On August 15, the Albany Common Council agreed to guarantee company bonds to the limit of $100,000 for the removal of the Schenectady plane. Within a month bidding was opened, and on October 15, 1842, a contract was negotiated with James and Charles Collins for $61,300, exclusive of land

the City, at or near the Hudson River, in such a manner as to dispense with the inclined plane."[18] Two days later, the Albany city lawmakers specified that the new track should follow "what is called the Patroon's Creek route" to the Hudson River.[19] When completed, double track ran from the foot of Maiden Lane adjacent to the river, westerly to intersect with the original line at what is now Fuller Road.[20]

In order to achieve the alternate route, the city fathers agreed to purchase the right-of-way and land for the depot, and lease them to the railroad until January 1, 1864 at a rent of 1 percent per year of the value at purchase. When the lease expired, the Mohawk and Hudson could buy the land from the city at its original purchase price. Another stipulation in the agreement was that at least one of the two tracks would be put down using the all-iron "H" rail.[21] The final cost of construction of the Patroon's Creek line, exclusive of land purchased, was nearly $202,000.[22]

With the opening of the new track that avoided the Albany plane on September 30, 1844, all original Mohawk and Hudson track in Albany was abandoned. (The Western Avenue to Capital Square line had ceased to be used three years earlier.[23]) This meant that the railroad also divested itself of its stationary steam engines and its horses, along with the two vexatious inclined planes.

Elimination of the inclined planes also served to demonstrate the cooperation between a private enterprise and a public municipality in order to over-

when it transported 2,096 tons from Albany and 870 tons from Schenectady.[24] The railroad's chief connection at the Albany end was with Hudson River traffic, but its western connection was potentially with both the Erie Canal and the Saratoga and Schenectady Railroad. Freight traffic from Saratoga County, the principal region served by the Saratoga and Schenectady, undoubtedly would be less than the trade from the vast area tapped by the Erie Canal.

In any case, the lopsided numbers for east-to-west movement for 1833 were reversed the following year. In 1834, the Mohawk and Hudson moved 5,282 tons of merchandise from Albany, but 11,313 tons were taken from Schenectady.[25] Of the tonnage bound for Schenectady, 1,891 tons, or roughly 35 percent, was

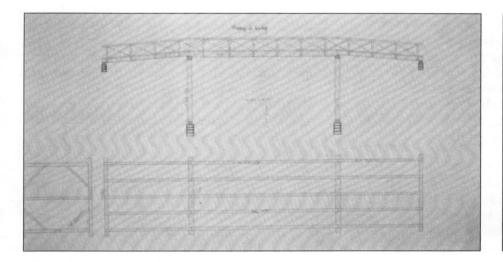

Railroad bridge plans—Saratoga and Schenectady. *Left:* Bridge at Curtiss'. *Right:* Swing bridge.
Courtesy of the Jervis Collection

come obstacles that were seen by both to be hindering the success of a mutually beneficial business. This, after all, was in accord with the "modernist" thinking of Whigs and conservative Democrats to maximize the value of the new technology. By working together, they believed, the Mohawk and Hudson Railroad and the business leaders of the City of Albany could help assure profits for all.

It seemed reasonable that the removal of the inclines would facilitate the movement of freight over the Mohawk and Hudson. Whether this benefit would follow remained to be seen. The state's earliest railroad was one of the few between the Hudson River and Lake Erie that did not have a charter restriction preventing it from freely moving freight. The Mohawk and Hudson began to do so in 1833,

transshipped west on the Erie Canal. Yet, a sum approaching half of the tonnage carried east on the railroad came from the canal. The collector of canal tolls at Schenectady recorded the amount and kind of freight passing between the Erie Canal and the Mohawk and Hudson Railroad and listed the specific articles that arrived via canal at Schenectady in 1834 that were then shipped east by rail. The items and quantities were:[26]

Item	Quantity	
domestic spirits	74,414	gallons
staves	76,640	in number
flour	73,178	barrels
provisions	673	"
ashes	936	"
cider	14	"
wood	21.5	cords
potatoes	1,280	bushels

dried fruit	1,779	pounds
clover and grass seed	61,914	"
flax seed	6,674	"
wool	11,471	"
cheese	4,271	"
butter and lard	11,571	"
hops	10,127	"
hemp	6,762	"
tobacco	21,569	"
furs and peltry	94,153	"
merchandize	2,606	"
furniture	18,243	"
bar and pig lead	10,000	"
sundries	182,066	"

The list exemplifies not only the freight moved on the Mohawk and Hudson in 1834, but also the goods that were coming out of the west at the time. Items that could not appear on the roster were gunpowder, friction matches, or like combustibles, which were not carried by the railroad "on any terms."[27]

Although canal freight transfers and material transferred from the Saratoga and Schenectady Railroad, and from the Utica and Schenectady following its opening in 1836, should have assured a substantial traffic in merchandise for the Mohawk and Hudson, this was not the case during the remainder of the 1830s. The total net profit from freight from 1833 through 1839 amounted to only $3,926.15.[28] The January 29, 1840, railroad superintendent's report that gave the dismal details listed freight rates at 62.5 cents per ton for merchandise received from the Erie Canal at Schenectady, $1 per ton for freight shipped by the residents of Schenectady, and $1.25 for each ton of goods transshipped from the Schenectady and Saratoga Railroad.[29]

The Mohawk and Hudson's directors who received the report were quick to react. They complained that the freight rate for cargo received from canal boats was only one-half the 8 cents per mile average of freight charges of "all railroads in the United States." The directors were incensed that the expenses of their freight storehouses amounted to more than one-third of the total freight expense of nearly $25,500 incurred in 1839. Then they bitterly noted that they had been led to believe by "the friends" of the move to put the railroad into the "carrying business" in 1833 that upwards of 70,000 tons of goods each year loaded from the canal alone would pass over the railroad. Since the total tonnage between 1833 and 1840 was only 144,897, the directors somewhat sarcastically pointed out that the 20,699 actual annual average tonnage was much less than had been projected.[30] Of course, the effects of the 1837 depression added to the tonnage shortfall.

Even though the directors recommended that the railroad occupy itself almost exclusively with the passenger trade, the Mohawk and Hudson continued to ship freight. By 1843, the economic hard times had run their course, yet the railroad's freight business failed to rebound. Freight revenue for the five years ending in 1847 accounted for only $98,969.14 out of a total income of $521,878.63. The road's net income for that period was $289,603, derived mainly from the passenger trade.[31]

But the 1850s started out much better, with freight income posting a substantial jump by 1852. The $117,859.94 gross freight revenue for that year was nearly 43 percent of the 1850–1852 total income for freight, and measured nearly 69 percent as large as the $171,753 taken in from passenger tickets for 1852.[32] On July 10, 1851, the New York Legislature abolished the payment of canal tolls by all railroads, effective the following December 1.[33] Undoubtedly, this caused an increase of the amount of goods shipped, and therefore boosted the Mohawk and Hudson's income from freight for 1852.

The Mohawk and Hudson's revenue expansion was not due to merchandise shipments alone. From 1850 to 1852, money derived from the passenger trade rose by over $39,500, or approximately $7,000 less than the increase in freight revenue. The total amount realized from passengers during the three-year span was $450,610, or slightly more than 60 percent of the railroad's total income for the same period. After deducting operating expenses, net income for 1850--1852 was a relatively healthy $418,019, the highest of any three-year period in the railroad's history. By then, the considerable increase in rail traffic between Albany and Buffalo was having a correspondingly favorable impact on the line that ran the first sixteen miles between the two cities.

Traffic increase by mid-century led the railroads to modernize their equipment. New locomotives were ordered and existing ones rebuilt to the latest 4-4-0 wheel arrangement that provided for two sets of drive wheels instead of one pair. The Mohawk and Hudson and the Saratoga and Schenectady had been at the leading edge of the previous technological change with the 4-2-0 design. John B. Jervis fashioned his Experiment in the 4-2-0 configuration and introduced it on the Mohawk and Hudson. It was quickly copied by locomotive builders, and Jervis himself used the Experiment as a template for the rebuilding of the English-made Robert Fulton (renamed John Bull), and the Davy Crockett of the Saratoga and Schenectady line. The Jervis-designed engines com-

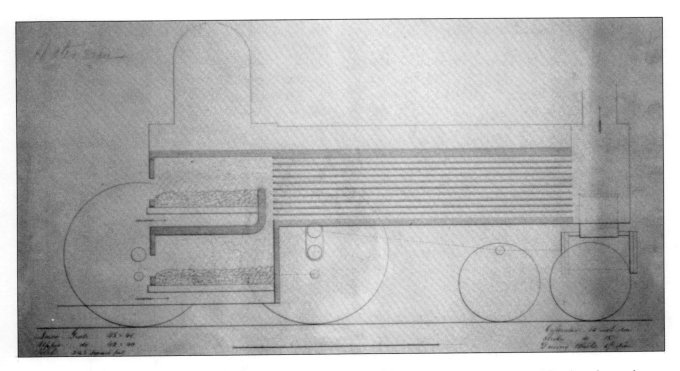

Plan for a 4-4-0 locomotive, possibly the rebuilt Experiment. It appears to have a two-tiered fire box for coal.
Courtesy of the Jervis Colleciton

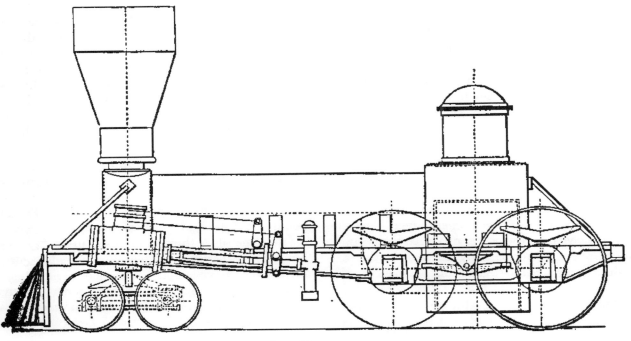

¼ in. = 1 foot.

The locomotive Mohawk as rebuilt to 4-4-0 wheel configuration.
From *Practical Mechanics Journal*, May, 1850

73

bined increased speed with a relatively smooth operating motion.

The Mohawk and Hudson added two more locomotives in 1834. The Mohawk and the Hudson were both built by Robert Stephenson and Sons with the 4-2-0 wheel arrangement. Their drive wheels were forty-eight inches in diameter and their cylinders ten inches by fourteen inches.[34] Possibly the last 4-2-0 locomotive purchased by the railroad was the Columbia. It was delivered in December 1841 from Rogers, Ketcham, and Grosvenor of Patterson, New Jersey, at a cost of $7,500 for the engine and tender. (At least that was the base price. The practice of add-ons apparently had started even at that early time, since the Mohawk and Hudson paid an extra $240 for a copper furnace (firebox) and $42.20 for "valves, flues, etc."[35])

The six-wheel engine, or "Jervis type," was the principal locomotive design built in the United States between 1835 and 1842. In fact, in 1840, nearly two-thirds of the engines produced had the 4-2-0 wheel plan.[36] But this was about to change in the '40s, and the Mohawk and Hudson was not to be left behind in obtaining the next generation of locomotives, the 4-4-0s.

The American type, or 4-4-0, "was the most popular wheel arrangement in nineteenth-century America." This engine design "succeeded because it met every requirement of early United States railroads." It was suited for all railway service, and "it was flexible, having three point suspension and a leading truck, . . .operated well on uneven tracks. . .was simple. . .low in first cost, and it was relatively powerful because of its four connected driving wheels."[37] Through the middle of the nineteenth century, locomotives on this design became progressively larger, although after the end of the Civil War weight and horsepower increases tended to level off.

As John White, Jr., pointed out in his history of American locomotive development, since "the locomotive is a vehicle, the power produced by its boiler and cylinders is only partially delivered to the rails by the driving wheels." As a result, "adhesion—the friction between the rail and the driving wheel tire attributable to the weight on the drivers—materially affects the pulling power of a locomotive."[38] As a rule, adhesion is estimated at one-fifth of the weight on the drive wheels. Using this calculation, a comparison of a typical 4-2-0 of the mid-1830s with a standard 4-4-0 in use a decade later can illustrate the 4-4-0's advantage. The earlier locomotive, weighing

ten tons—of which four tons were on the driving wheels—had an adhesion of 1,600 pounds, whereas the 4-4-0 engine of the middle 1840s, weighing eighteen tons—with twelve tons over the drivers—had a 4,800 pounds adhesion, or three times that of the earlier locomotive. The addition of an extra pair of drivers, arranged to bring two-thirds of the increased locomotive weight to bear on the drivers, produced a proportionally greater advantage over the earlier engine's configuration, which placed only a little more than one-third the total weight on the driving wheels.

Horsepower and tractive effort (pulling power of a locomotive) also increased by the 1840s with the enlargement of the bore and stroke of cylinders. The increase of boiler heating surface and the resultant rise in steam pressure contributed to the boost in power and tractive effort, as well.

Probably the first 4-4-0 machine acquired by the Mohawk and Hudson was the Noah Vibbard. Said to have been built in 1840 by the mechanical wizard David Matthew, its cylinders measured sixteen inches by twenty inches and its wheels were an impressive sixty-six inches in diameter.[39] If Matthew built the machine in 1840, he did so while employed as locomotive superintendent by the Utica and Schenectady Railroad.[40] The same Mohawk and Hudson historian who attributed the Noah Vibbard to David Matthew wrote that the railroad also "purchased ten or eleven other 4-4-0 locomotives during the late 1840s and 1850s. . . ."[41] Undoubtedly the company bought more machines of the new wheel arrangement, built at least one named the Mechanic at its own shops, and also rebuilt some of its older 4-2-0s.[42]

The man who supervised much of the rebuilding was Walter McQueen, the Mohawk and Hudson's master mechanic from 1845 to 1850. His first rebuild was the John Bull. Originally the Robert Fulton when it arrived from England as a 0-4-0 in 1831, it became the John Bull when transformed into a 4-2-0. At the time of its third incarnation in 1845, it was renamed Rochester. The following year, McQueen made over the venerable Experiment. The pioneer locomotive's cylinders were increased to twelve inches by eighteen inches and its two drivers, measuring sixty inches in diameter, were replaced by four, each with a diameter of fifty-four inches.[43]

Another McQueen rebuild was the Mohawk, done at the company shops in 1848. It was given drive wheels sixty inches in diameter and cylinders that were fifteen inches in diameter, with a stroke of twenty-five inches.[44] But the most significant technological improvement added to the Mohawk was a "saddle" to hold the cylinders, enabling their attachment to the frame. The "most secure form of cylinder fastening was direct bolting to the frame" of the locomotive. This was accomplished "with a bed plate called a 'saddle' which can be firmly attached between the frame under the smokebox."[45] The Mohawk and Hudson's Mohawk is regarded as "the earliest engine with a cylinder saddle."[46]

The Mohawk and Hudson Railroad entered the second half of the nineteenth century with locomotives that were up-to-date and sufficiently powerful to meet the needs of the increased traffic and greater loads. But, the size and wheel arrangement of locomotives were not the only transformations to occur to the Mohawk and Hudson during the 1850s. Churchill C. Cambreling's predictive toast made two decades earlier was soon to come true. The Buffalo connection was about to profoundly affect the railroad from Albany to Schenectady just as it had, in a way, already impacted the railroad from Schenectady to Saratoga.

This 1905 map shows the railroads that combined to form the New York Central plus the Saratoga and Schenectady. It also shows New York's canal system.

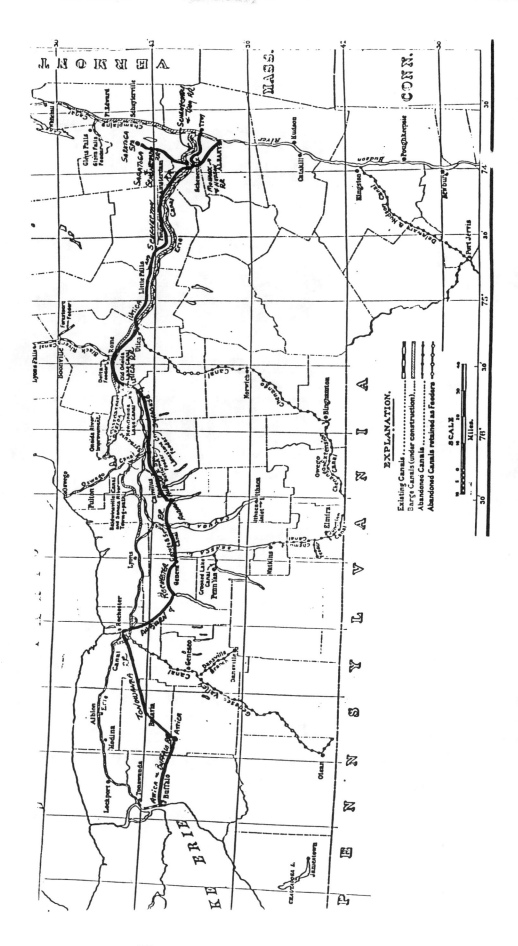

75

SINGLE MEALS 25 CENTS,

AT THE

RAIL-ROAD EXCHANGE,

Entrance Nos. 25 & 27 Maiden Lane,

Fronting on Broadway, Albany.

This House adjoins the square used as a Depot by the Mohawk and Hudson Rail Road Company, and opposite the Ticket Office of the Boston Rail Road, and contiguous to the Steamboat Landings.

☞ A Licensed Porter always in attendance.

Board and Lodging, by the Day or Week, on reasonable terms.

ABNER A. POND.

VIII: The Buffalo Railroad

In 1843, posters appeared along the lines of the several railroads between Albany and Buffalo advertising a through connection between the two cities. It was announced that beginning July 10, three trains daily would move passengers both east and west across the state. The posters optimistically proclaimed that the 326 miles between the Hudson River and Lake Erie would be made "through in 25 hours." First class fare would cost $10, second class $8, and emigrants would be carried "only by special contract."[1] Congressman Cambreling's earlier prediction was about to become a reality.

The through connection was made possible with the completion of the Attica and Buffalo line by the beginning of 1843, followed by a January 31 meeting of the delegates representing the eight railroads constructed between the Hudson and Lake Erie.[2] The run from Albany to Buffalo required only one change of railroads, since a connection was lacking at Rochester between the Auburn and Rochester and the Tonowanda Railroad.[3]

Agreement among the various railroads and the advertisements notwithstanding, there were several problems to surmount in order to make the arrangement work. Coordinating traffic over the many roads was, in itself, daunting. For example, only the recently opened Schenectady and Troy was built with iron rails; all the others still used wooden rails topped with thin iron straps. This situation could force the average speed below the thirteen miles per hour plus needed to make the advertisedtwenty-five-hour trip time. Of course, the thirteen miles per hour average needed to make the run apparently did not take into consideration the time consumed by stops. But this may have been among the least concerns, considering that in 1843 railroads had "no telegraph system, no signal system, no air brakes for controlling fast and heavy trains," and no dining cars. Lack of diners meant that travelers had to scramble to seek food at station restaurants during stops to pick up or discharge passengers.[4]

Another problem that the central New York lines attempted to solve was that of winter travel. It was agreed "that during the winter months the train shall leave Buffalo at 7 in the morning and reach and remain over night at Syracuse; and leave Albany at 9 in the morning and stay over night at Auburn; so that a passenger may make the passage between Albany and Buffalo in two days."[5] Anyone who has traveled between the two cities in the winter, particularly along the stretch west of Utica, can well appreciate the reason for the schedule.

Another accommodation to passenger safety and comfort that was included in the 1843 pact was the resolution "that the several companies upon the Rail Road line will not employ persons in the business of transportation who ever drink intoxicating liquors."[6] Exactly how this would be enforced, especially regarding off-duty trainmen, was not explained.

Apparently the Mohawk and Hudson, and even the Saratoga and Schenectady, were urged by the Utica and Schenectady, their western connection, to make the arrangement for through travel work as smooth as possible. The executive committee of the latter railroad was authorized to confer with the two other lines about the erection of a depot in Schenectady for the mutual accommodation of all three railroad companies.[7] The construction of a "union" station would assist in the more rapid movement of passengers.

Modernization in the form of iron rails came to the Mohawk and Hudson and the other roads across central New York in the 1840s. John B. Jervis lobbied for the all-iron rail at the time the Mohawk and Hudson was under construction. The immediate cost worked against the long-range savings that should have occurred, and the iron rails were not used. As a result, the Schenectady and Troy became the first of the railroads in the Hudson River to Lake Erie crossing to use them, not the Mohawk and Hudson. The Schenectady and Troy also was the Mohawk and

Hudson's major competitor when the former line was opened in 1842.

By the mid-1840s, both the Utica and Schenectady and the Syracuse and Utica commenced to relay their track with the improved heavy iron rail. In 1844, shortly before those two railroads went to iron rails, the Mohawk and Hudson put down iron "H" rail on the Patroon's Creek route that eliminated the Albany inclined plane. Then, in 1847, the New York Legislature passed a bill which, in effect, forced "any railroad company whose track is now laid in whole or in part with the flat bar rail on which steam power is used in propelling cars" to replace the old rail. The railroads between Albany and Buffalo were given until 1850 to make the change or forfeit their charter.[8] The various roads made the required change, with the Mohawk and Hudson completing its rail replacement by 1849 with iron rail weighing sixty-three pounds to the yard.[9] The new iron rails apparently had a positive effect on through travel; in 1849, of the six daily trains that left Albany for Buffalo, the fastest trip was made in fifteen hours.[10]

Left, top: Cross section of iron "U" rail, a form used in early, all-iron rail. Author's collection

Left middle: Side view of "U" rail showing indentation along the top made by wheel flanges. Author's collection

Left bottom: Top view of "U" rail (sometimes called bridge rail). Author's collection

Below: Plan of wrought iron rail chair to fasten iron rail to ties. Courtesy of the Jervis Collection

Another act that passed the legislature in 1847 was one initiated by the Mohawk and Hudson. The legislation permitted the railroad to change its name to the Albany and Schenectady Railroad Company. The reason behind the name alteration is obscure, but it could have been to bring the company more in conformation with the other cross-state lines. All but one used community designations in their corporate names. At a time when greater cooperation was occurring, the Mohawk and Hudson might have felt it advantageous to direct attention to the fact that their railroad connected the cities of Albany and Schenectady, not simply the Hudson and Mohawk Rivers.

The agreement among the railroads across central New York and the installation of new iron rails both worked toward facilitating the fifteen-hour fastest time crossing between Albany and Buffalo. This was acceptable for a while, but there was little doubt that in the long run a more satisfactory arrangement was needed. Competition dictated the change. By 1850, there were twenty-nine railroads in New York already built or under construction.[11] It was only a matter of time before a single railroad crossed the state from the Hudson River to Lake Erie. That railroad was completed the next year.

On May 14, 1851, a ceremonial train chugged westward over the recently completed New York and Erie Railroad. Engineered by Benjamin Wright, Horatio Allen, and others and nearly twenty years in the making, the road ran from Piermont, on the west bank of the Hudson about twenty-five miles north of New York City, across New York's southern tier to Dunkirk on Lake Erie, some thirty-five miles south of Buffalo. At the time, the 483-mile line was the longest railroad in the United States.

It was fitting that the first official train carried among its passengers a high-ranking son of western New York, President Millard Fillmore, along with Secretary of State Daniel Webster and three other cabinet members.[12] The president and his cabinet members could join in the rejoicing that, at last, a single iron road connected the mighty Hudson River near its outlet at New York harbor with the Great Lakes. But the celebrating was far from universal. The officers and stockholders of the several small lines between Albany and Buffalo, the rechristened Albany and Schenectady among them, could only speculate on the extent of competitive damage that might occur from the new line. And the Erie was not the only railroad to connect the Atlantic coastal areas with the hinterland: The Pennsylvania Railroad was built to Pittsburg (therefore the Ohio River) in 1852, and the Baltimore and Ohio was opened to the Ohio River in 1853.

Three months before the ceremonial train rolled along the Erie tracks to Dunkirk, a convention of all the central New York companies was held at Albany. Erastus Corning, president of the Utica and Schenectady and prominent Albany entrepreneur,[13] took the lead with a motion "that a Committee consisting of the Presidents of each Company on the main line between Albany and Buffalo, be appointed to make application at the present session of the Legislature for a law authorizing any two or more Companies on this Line to consolidate their stock and become one Company" if the stockholders owning two-thirds of the securities of the companies involved supported the merger. Corning's resolution was unanimously adopted on February 12.[14] Still, another two years passed before the concept became a reality.

If the perceived impending doom resulting from the completion of the New York and Erie and the other lines to the Ohio River helped spur cooperation between the Albany and Schenectady and the other roads to the west, another event in 1851 must have engendered some optimism. On October 1, the Hudson River Railroad arrived at East Greenbush, across the river from Albany.[15] This was one more reason for the various railroads to cooperate, because the Hudson River Railroad was the upstate rail tie to New York City.

Chartered in 1846 and constructed by the ubiquitous engineer John B. Jervis, the Hudson River Railroad was an ice-free link to Albany that enabled the great port metropolis 140 miles south "to tap into a line of upstate railroads which ran west to Buffalo."[16] The New York City to Albany to Buffalo connection was expanded to the Mississippi during the 1850s, making New York City "the chief Atlantic terminus of the expanding national railroad network,"[17] and therefore bringing increased traffic to the railroads between Albany and Buffalo.

Obviously, the Albany and Schenectady benefitted because its traffic, particularly freight, was mostly through, not local. The movement of merchandise increased markedly in 1852 and 1853, the years immediately prior to consolidation of all the Albany-to-Buffalo lines. If calculated in density per mile tons (the average number of tons carried over one mile of road), the Albany and Schenectady's total for 1851 was 92,058. The following year the density per mile tons jumped to 162,178 and in the first ten months of 1853 alone the total climbed to 205,886.[18] While the freight traffic increase could be attributed chiefly to the legislature's elimination of the payment of canal tolls by railroads effective December 1, 1851, the Hudson River Railroad connection to New York City also contributed to the Albany and Schenectady's prosperity. Yet, the rise in business notwithstanding, New York's first railroad still found it necessary to join with the other roads to the west in order to survive in the railroad-building frenzy of the 1850s.

Finally, a special act of the state legislature effective April 2, 1853, permitted the consolidation of two or more of the railroad companies between the Hudson River and Lake Erie that were specifically named in the legislation. The Albany and Schenectady Railroad headed the list.[19] There were 277 people who owned stock in the Albany and Schenectady on the date of the legislation. This was a little less than 10 percent of the total stockholders representing the eight lines that took part in the merger.[20]

Erastus Corning.
Library of Congress

Once the consolidation law was passed, the railroads moved quickly to achieve the desired goal. On April 4, the Albany and Schenectady chose a committee composed of President Ezekial C. McIntosh and Directors Thomas Tileston, R. H. Winslow, and H. Pumpelly, to represent the company at the initial merger talks held in Syracuse on April 12.[21] During the next three months, additional meetings were held to iron out details, the most vexatious of which was the formula by which stock in the old companies would be exchanged for stock in the new corporation. The resolution provided for Albany and Schenectady stock to be received at a rate of 117. The shareholders acquired stock in the new corporation at par, with the difference made up in thirty-year 6 percent bonds.[22]

The stockholders of the Albany and Schenectady Railroad unanimously ratified the agreement, as did those of the other railroads, on June 29. On July 7, 1853, Erastus Corning was elected president of the new railroad, along with a vice president and a secretary treasurer to help him manage the new company. With this action, the New York Central Railroad

officially came into existence.[23] Finally, a single line spanned the distance from Albany to Buffalo. The organization of the New York Central also meant that the state's first railroad—the Mohawk and Hudson/Albany and Schenectady—surrendered its corporate identity after twenty-two years of operation.

The Saratoga and Schenectady, the second railroad in New York, also lost its corporate individuality by the 1850s. In the spring of 1836, the Rensselaer and Saratoga Railroad had opened from Troy to Ballston Spa.[24] In October 1850, the Rensselaer and Saratoga gained entry into the village of Saratoga Springs by negotiating a fifteen-year lease of the Saratoga and Schenectady, effective January 1, 1851.[25] Nine years later, Saratoga and Schenectady President L. G. B. Cannon signed away the railroad operations of his company when he agreed to a permanent lease by the Rensselaer and Saratoga, effective July 1, 1860.[26]

Thus ended the autonomous operations of the two earliest railroads in New York. The Mohawk and Hudson and the Saratoga and Schenectady functioned independently for roughly two decades. This was a limited life span, but their pioneer railroading accomplishments were considerable. Both of these early transportation companies could list among their achievements the fact that they were built specifically to employ the use of locomotives; they introduced the first engines designed with moveable or swivel lead trucks; they exemplified the exchange of technology between Great Britain and the United States; and they were among the earliest, if not the first, railroads in the nation to use wooden cross ties in track construction.

This is an impressive record for two short-line railroads. Yet, today almost nothing remains of the initial construction to serve as testimony to their contributions to the transportation industry. Only a few hundred feet of the Mohawk and Hudson's earliest roadbed remains overgrown on the sandy plain of pine and scrub oak in west Albany. Even this fragile monument is in danger of obliteration by the encroachment of late twentieth century business expansion. It is ironic that this early line that promoted and sought to prosper from the movement of people and the associated growth of commercial enterprise now faces complete eradication at the hands of those entities to which it contributed so much.

During a recent trip on the Erie Canal, this author heard occasional horn blasts from locomotives pulling trains along the former New York Central tracks, now used by Amtrack. It was as if the engines were telling the canal boat not to give up on the old transportation links that helped build the state and the nation. Perhaps the railroads should take heart from an article in a recent issue of *Smithsonian*. Writing on the subject of freight trains, Per Ola and Emily d'Aulaire confidently declare that the "rail freight industry is alive and well and clearly on the move." The article ends with a quote from a sign in a railroad office in Cheyenne, Wyoming, that proclaims "There is no end of the line for railroad people."[27]

The excited passengers on that epochal trip in the summer of 1831 undoubtedly would agree.

Remaining original Mohawk and Hudson roadbed, Albany.
Author's collection

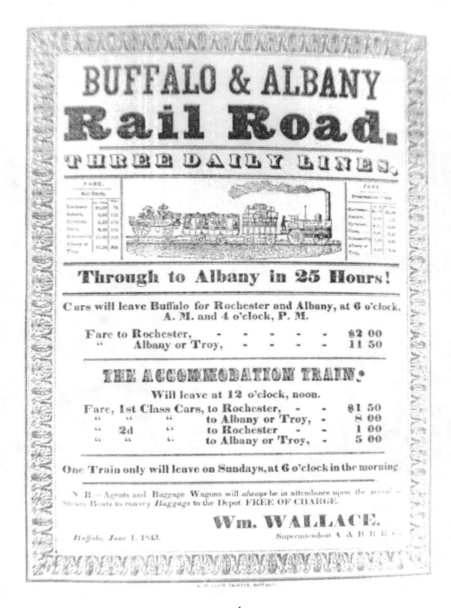

From: Stevens, *The Beginnings of the New York Central Railroad*.

Notes

I: The Land of Railroads

1. Nicholas Faith, *The World Railways Made*, New York: Carroll and Graf, 1991, 11.
2. Ibid., 12.
3. F. Daniel Larkin, *John B. Jervis: An American Engineering Pioneer*, Ames, Iowa: Iowa State University Press, 1990, 28.
4. Manville B. Wakefield, *Coal Boats to Tidewater*, Fleischmanns, NY: Purple Mountain Press, 1992, 2.
5. Wakefield, *Coal Boats*, 3-4.
6. Larkin, *John B. Jervis*, 16-18.
7. Ibid., 21.
8. Ibid.
9. Ibid., 25.
10. Ibid., 26-27.
11. Ibid.
12. Ibid., 29-30.
13. Ibid., 30.
14. Ibid.
15. Ibid., 30-31.
16. Ibid., 31. America's cylinder is in the Smithsonian Institution
17. John H. White, Jr., *A History of the American Locomotive: Its Development 1830-1880*, New York: Dover Publications, 1979, 242.
18. Ibid., 7.
19. Ibid., 243.
20. Ibid., 242.
21. Faith, *Railways*, 14.
22. Ibid.
23. Ibid., 15.
24. Brian Hollingsworth, *The Illustrated Encyclopedia of the World's Steam Passenger Locomotives*, London: Salamader Books, 1982, 18.
25. Ibid., 18-19.

II: The Beginnings

1. Noble E. Whitford, *History of the Canal System of the State of New York*, Albany: Brandow Printing Company, 1906, I: 123-26.
2. Frank W. Stevens, *The Beginnings of the New York Central Railroad*, New York: G.P. Putnam's Sons, 1926, 1.
3. Ibid., 397.
4. John DeMis, "Location of the Original Route of the Mohawk and Hudson Railroad," Unpublished master's thesis, New York State Library.
5. Ibid., 28-29.
6. Stevens, *New York Central*, 2.
7. Joel Munsell, "The Mohawk and Hudson Railroad," *Transactions of the Albany Institute*, 1876, VIII: 269-270.
8. DeMis, "Mohawk and Hudson," 30-31.
9. Ibid., 32.
10. Stevens, *New York Central*, 24-25.
11. Ibid., 26.
12. Ibid., 8.
13. DeMis, "Mohawk and Hudson," 35.
14. Stevens, *New York Central*, 56.
15. DeMis, "Mohawk and Hudson," 35.
16. Stevens, *New York Central*, 57.
17. DeMis, "Mohawk and Hudson," 32.
18. William M. Cushman, Engineer, *Report made to the President and Directors of the Albany and Schenectady Turnpike Company, upon laying a Rail Road upon their Turnpike*, August, 1831. The fifteen-page report contained estimates of excavations, materials, and the cost for a single and double track railroad.
19. Stevens, *New York Central*, 57-58.
20. DeMis, "Mohawk and Hudson," 42.
21. Stevens, *New York Central*, 58-59.
22. DeMis, "Mohawk and Hudson," 46-47.
23. Stevens, *New York Central*, 60.
24. DeMis, "Mohawk and Hudson," 46.
25. Stevens, *New York Central*, 61.
26. Ibid.
27. Fred B. Abele, *The Mohawk and Hudson Railroad Co., 1826-1853*, Schenectady, NY: Mohawk and Hudson Chapter, NRHS, 1981, 9 and 11.
28. *Albany Gazette*, July 23, 1833.
29. *Albany Gazette*, August 8, 1833.
30. *Albany Gazette*, November 20, 1833.
31. Ibid.
32. Ibid.
33. Stevens, *New York Central*, 62-63.

III. Construction

1. John F. Stover, *American Railroads*, Chicago: University of Chicago Press, 1961, 14-19.
2. Stevens, *New York Central*, 8.
3. Ibid., 12.
4. DeMis, "Mohawk and Hudson," 36-37.
5. Ibid., 38-40.
6. Ibid., 41.
7. Stevens, *New York Central*, 9.
8. Ibid., 6.
9. The new board included: John Jacob Astor, Lynde Catlin, James Duane, George W. Featherstonhaugh, Nicholas Fish, Peter A. Jay, David S. Jones, Herman LeRoy, and Stephen Van Rensselaer. Van Rensselaer was elected president, Featherstonhaugh, vice president, Catlin, treasurer, and Jay, secretary. Apparently, Featherstonhaugh was still the driving force in the company.
10. *New York Daily Advertiser*, February 12, 1829.
11. *Albany Gazette*, February 27, 1829.
12. Stevens, *New York Central*, 16-17.
13. *Albany Gazette*, February 27, 1829.
14. Stevens, *New York Central*, 18-19.
15. Ibid., 20-21.
16. Ibid.
17. Larkin, *John B. Jervis*, 158. n. 50.
18. Ibid., 36 and 38.
19. DeWitt S. Bloodgood, "Some Account of the Hudson and Mohawk Railroad," *The American Journal of Science and Arts*, XXI, January 1832, 142.
20. John B. Jervis, "Report to the President and Board of Managers of the Mohawk and Hudson Rail Road," July 20, 1830, Jervis MSS.
21. Ibid., 1-2.
22. Ibid., 3-7.
23. Ibid., 2.
24. Ibid., 20.
25. Ibid., 7-8.
26. John B. Jervis, "Report to the President and Managers of the Mohawk and Hudson Railroad Company," November 9, 1830, 2, Jervis MSS.
27. Ibid., 11.
28. Ibid., 13-18.
29. Ibid., 19-21.
30. Bloodgood, "Hudson and Mohawk Railroad," 142.
31. Neal FitzSimons, ed., *The Reminiscences of John B. Jervis: Engineer of the Old Croton*, Syracuse, NY: Syracuse University Press, 1971, 106.
32. Abele, *Mohawk and Hudson*, 8.
33. Jervis, "Report to the President and Board of Managers of the Mohawk and Hudson Railroad, July 20, 183, 9.
34. Ibid., 11.
35. Letter to an unknown individual from John B. Jervis, Feb. 14, 1831. Jervis MSS.
36. Bloodgood, "Hudson and Mohawk Railroad," 143.
37. John B. Jervis, "Historical Sketch of the Mohawk and Hudson Railroad," 1. Jervis MSS.
38. Ibid., 2.
39. Larkin, *John B. Jervis*, 39-40.
40. Ibid., 41.
41. John B. Jervis to C.C. Cambreling, Oct. 1, 1831. Jervis MSS.
42. Ibid.
43. Ibid.
44. Ibid.
45. Larkin, *John B. Jervis*, 41.
46. Stevens, *New York Central*, 31.
47. Bloodgood, "Hudson and Mohawk Railroad," 144.
48. Ibid.
49. Ibid., 145.
50. Ibid., 146.
51. Roger E. Carp, "The Erie Canal and the Liberal Challenge to Classical Republicanism, 1785-1850," Unpublished PhD dissertation, 1986, University Microfilms Incorporated, 799.
52. Abele, *Mohawk and Hudson*, 11.
53. Ibid., 7.
54. Ibid.
55. Joel Munsell, *Annals of Albany*, Albany: Munsell and Rowland, 1858, IX: 261.
56. Ibid., 248.

IV: The First Trains

1. Munsell, "Mohawk and Hudson," 278.
2. William H. Brown, *The History of the First Locomotives in America*, New York: D. Appleton and Company, 1871, 176-177.
3. Ibid. Travel from Albany to Buffalo in 1831 averaged 72 non-stop hours by stage coach.
4. Mohawk and Hudson Document signed E. L. H. contained in the Mohawk and Hudson Collection at the Albany Institute of History and Art.
5. Brown, *First Locomotives*, 179-180.
6. Ibid., 180.
7. Ibid.
8. Ibid.
9. *Albany Gazette*, August 19, 1831.
10. *Albany Gazette*, August 23, 1831.
11. *Albany Gazette*, July 29, 1831.
12. Contracts for Locomotive and Stationary Engine, March 15, 1831. Jervis MSS.
13. Contract for Waggon Wheels, April 4, 1831 and Contract for Wooden Wheels, May 6, 1831. Jervis MSS.
14. Brown, *First Locomotives*, 178.

15. Bloodgood, *Hudson and Mohawk Rail-Road*, 147.
16. Ibid., 148.
17. Larkin, *John B. Jervis*, 42.
18. Railway and Locomotive Historical Society, Bulletin #55, May 1941, 24.
19. Ibid., 25.
20. *The American Journal of Science and Arts*, XXI, Jan. 1832, 385-86.
21. Stevens, *Mohawk and Hudson*, 37.
22. Larkin, *John B. Jervis*, 42.
23. Ibid., 42-43.
24. Ibid., 43. A Clinton drive wheel is in the Smithsonian Institution.
25. Jervis, Report to the President of the Mohawk and Hudson, November 9, 1830.
26. Ibid.
27. Ibid.
28. Bloodgood, *Hudson and Mohawk*, 148.
29. Ibid.
30. Larkin, *John B. Jervis*, 41.
31. "Locomotive by Stevenson" [sic], July 5, 1831, Jervis MSS.
32. Ibid.
33. Ibid.
34. Stevens, *New York Central*, 111-112.
35. Larkin, *John B. Jervis*, 43.
36. Ibid.
37. Ibid., 44.
38. Articles of Agreement between the West Point Foundry Association and the Mohawk and Hudson Railroad Company, November 16, 1831. Jervis MSS.
39. Ibid.
40. Ibid.
41. Ibid.
42. Ibid.
43. Larkin, *John B. Jervis*, 44-45.
44. Ibid., 45.
45. Ibid.
46. Ibid.
47. Thomas Tredgold, *A Practical Treatise on Railroads and Carriages*, London: Josiah Taylor, 1825, 94 and 179.
48. Larkin, *John B. Jervis*, 47.
49. Ibid.
50. Ibid.
51. Ibid., 48.
52. Ibid.
53. Ibid.
54. Ibid.
55. Ibid.
56. Ibid.
57. Ibid., 49.
58. White, *American Locomotive*, 34.

V: Another Railroad

1. *Report of the Committee on the Affairs of the Saratoga and Schenectady Railroad*, New York: Sleight and Van Norden, 1833, 13-14.
2. Ibid., 15-19.
3. Ibid., 29.
4. Ibid., 32.
5. Larkin, *John B. Jervis*, 49.
6. Ibid.
7. Friends of William C. Young, *Biography of William C. Young*, New York: Styles and Cash, 1889, 25-26.
8. *American Railroad Journal*, May 11, 1833.
9. Ibid.
10. *American Railroad Journal*, April 6, 1833.
11. *American Railway Journal*, May 11, 1833.
12. Ibid.
13. Ibid.
14. Alvin F. Harlow. *The Road of the Century: The Story of the New York Central*. New York: Creative Age Press, Inc., 1947, 20.
15. *American Railroad Journal*, July 27, 1833.
16. Ibid.
17. Ibid.
18. Undated notation in Mohawk and Hudson Letterbook, Jervis MSS.
19. *American Railroad Journal*, July 27, 1833.
20. *American Railroad Journal*, August 3, 1833.
21. *American Railroad Journal*, July 6, 1832.
22. Ibid.
23. Ibid.
24. *American Railroad Journal*, July 27, 1833.
25. John H. White, Jr. *American Locomotives: An Engineering History, 1830-1880*, Baltimore: Johns Hopkins Press, 1968, 34.
26. *American Railroad Journal*, July 27, 1833.
27. *Albany Gazette*, July 29, 1831.
28. Ulysses P. Hedrick, *A History of Agriculture in the State of New York*, New York: Hill & Wang, 1966, 187.
29. Abele, *Mohawk and Hudson*, 18.
30. Mohawk and Hudson Document Signed E.L.H.
31. Larkin, *John B. Jervis*, 43.
32. *American Railroad Journal*, July 20, 1833.
33. Ibid.
34. Stevens, *New York Central*, 55.
35. Ibid.

VI: Running Railroads

1. Stevens, *New York Central*, 55.
2. Report of John B. Jervis to the President and Directors of the Mohawk and Hudson Railroad, Jan., 30, 1833. Jervis MSS.

3. Ibid.
4. White, *American Locomotives*, 212.
5. Jervis to the President of the Mohawk and Hudson, January 30, 1833.
6. Ibid.
7. Ibid.
8. Ibid.
9. Abele, *Mohawk and Hudson*, 9.
10. Jervis to the President of the Mohawk and Hudson, January 30, 1833.
11. Ibid.
12. Ibid.
13. Ibid.
14. Ibid.
15. Ibid.
16. Ibid.
17. Ibid.
18. Ibid.
19. Ibid.
20. Ronald E. Shaw, *Erie Water West*, Lexington: Univ. of Kentucky Press, 1966, 287.
21. Jervis to the President of the Mohawk and Hudson, January 30, 1833.
22. Ibid.
23. Mohawk and Hudson Company Minutes, vol. 253, New York Public Library.
24. Stevens, *New York Central*, 100-101.
25. David Ellis et al., *A History of New York State*, Ithaca: Cornell University Press, 1967, 251.
26. Stevens, *New York Central*, 268.
27. Noble E. Whitford, *History of the Canal System of the State of New York*, Albany: Brandow Printing, 1906. II: 1069.
28. Annual Account of the Property..., Utica & Schenectady Railroad, Box D7613, NYS Archives.
29. John DeMis, "Mohawk and Hudson," 80-81.
30. Ibid., 72.
31. Ibid., 71-72.
32. Ibid., 74.
33. Statement of Receipts of Saratoga and Schenectady Railroad to 1st August, 1839, Mohawk and Hudson Papers, Albany Institute of History and Art.
34. Ibid.
35. List of Persons Employed by the Mohawk and Hudson Railroad Company, June 1839, Mohawk and Hudson Papers, Albany Institute of History and Art.
36. Ibid.
37. Ibid.
38. Ibid.
39. White, *American Locomotives*, 21.
40. Abele, *Mohawk and Hudson*, 19.
41. Ibid.
42. Journal of General Affairs of the Mohawk and Hudson Railroad Company, 1839-1843, 62, New York State Library.
43. Ibid.
44. Ibid., 51-59.
45. Ibid., 79.
46. George R. McLaughlin to the President of the Albany and Schenectady Railroad Company, December 9, 1840, Mohawk and Hudson Papers, Albany Institute of History and Art.
47. Bank of Troy to General John E. Wool, October 30, 1835, Box 7, Folder 5, General John E. Wool MSS.

VII: Competition and Cooperation

1. Shaw, *Erie Water West*, 289.
2. Ibid., 216.
3. Whitford, *Canal System*, Vol. I, 914.
4. M. T. Reynolds to David Wood, President of the Mohawk and Hudson Railroad, September 15, 1840, Mohawk and Hudson Papers, Albany Institute of History and Art.
5. Ibid.
6. Ibid.
7. Journal of General Affairs of the Mohawk and Hudson, 1839-1843, 72.
8. M. T. Reynolds to David Wood, Sept. 15, 1840.
9. Ibid.
10. Ibid.
11. DeMis, "Location of the Original Route," 60.
12. Stevens, *New York Central*, 71.
13. Abele, *Mohawk and Hudson*, 11.
14. Stevens, *New York Central*, 72.
15. Ibid., 77-79.
16. Ibid., 79.
17. Abele, *Mohawk and Hudson*, 11.
18. Ibid., 80-81.
19. Ibid.
20. Ibid.
21. Stevens, *New York Central*, 83.
22. Ibid., 85.
23. Abele, *Mohawk and Hudson*, 11.
24. Stevens, *New York Central*, 89.
25. Ibid.
26. DeMis, "Location of Original Route," 92.
27. Ibid., 86.
28. Stevens, *New York Central*, 89.
29. Ibid., 90.
30. Ibid., 90-91.
31. Ibid., 102.
32. Ibid., 103.
33. Ibid., 273.
34. Abele, *Mohawk and Hudson*, 19.
35. Journal of General Affairs of the Mohawk and Hudson, 131.

36. White, *American Locomotives*, 33.
37. Ibid., 46.
38. Ibid., 74-75.
39. Abele, *Mohawk and Hudson*, 19.
40. White, *American Locomotives*, 455.
41. Abele, *Mohawk and Hudson*, 19.
42. White, *American Locomotives*, 454.
43. Ibid., 45.
44. Ibid., 51-53.
45. Ibid., 207.
46. Ibid., 454.

VIII: The Buffalo Railroad

1. *Railway Passenger Travel*, Maynard, Mass.: Chandler Press, 1987, 7.
2. The railroads in east-to-west order were the: Mohawk and Hudson; Schenectady and Troy; Utica and Schenectady; Syracuse and Utica; Auburn and Syracuse; Auburn and Rochester; Tonawanda; and the Attica and Buffalo.
3. Stevens, *New York Central*, 317-21.
4. Ibid., 321-22.
5. Ibid., 323.
6. Ibid.
7. Undated Utica and Schenectady resolution in Mohawk and Hudson papers, Albany Institute of History and Art.
8. Stevens, *New York Central*, 298-99.
9. Ibid., 300.
10. Shaw, *Erie Water West*, 289.
11. J. H. French, *Gazetteer of the State of New York*, Syracuse: R.P. Smith, 1860, 66-74.
12. F. Daniel Larkin, "Erie Railroad," in Robert L. Frey (ed.), *Railroads in the Nineteenth Century, Encyclopedia of American Business History and Biography*, New York: Bruccoli Clark Layman, 1988, 115-16.
13. F. Daniel Larkin, "Erastus Corning," in Robert L. Frey (ed.), *Railroads in the Nineteenth Century, Encyclopedia of American Business History and Biography*, New York: Bruccoli Clark Layman, 1988, 65, 69.
14. Stevens, *New York Central*, 351.
15. Edward Hungerford, *Men and Iron: The Histor of the New York Central*, New York: Thomas Y. Crowell, 1938, 149.
16. Edward K. Spann, *The Metropolis: New York City 1840-1857*, New York: Columbia University Press, 1981, 14.
17. Ibid.
18. Stevens, *New York Central*, 275.
19. Ibid., 358-59.
20. Ibid., 352.
21. Ibid., 361-62.
22. French, *Gazetteer*, 69.
23. Ibid., 375. When the railroad company was organized in 1833, Corning became a director of the Utica and Schenectady. Of course, he eventually became president of the railroad. Also in 1833, he was elected a director of the Mohawk and Hudson. At the same time, he was named Mohawk and Hudson vice president, a post he held for two years. See: Irene D. Neu, *Erastus Corning: Merchant and Financier, 1794-1872*, Ithaca, N.Y.: Cornell University Press, 1960.
24. Ibid., 72.
25. *The Act of Incorporation of the Rensselaer and Saratoga Railroad Company*, New York: Evening Post Steam Presses, 1872.
26. Ibid.
27. Per Ola and Emily d'Aulaire, "Freight Trains are Back and They're On a Roll," *Smithsonian*, June 1995, Vol. 26, No. 3, 49.

Bibliography

Manuscript Collections

Jervis, John B. MSS. Jervis Public Library, Rome, NY.

Mohawk and Hudson Papers. Albany Institute of History and Art, Albany, NY.

Mohawk and Hudson Papers. New York Public Library, New York, NY.

Wool, John E. MSS. New York State Library, Albany, NY.

Public Documents

Cushman, William M. *Report Made to the President and Directors of the Albany and Schenectady Turnpike Company, Upon Laying a Rail Road Upon Their Turnpike.* 1931.

Report of the Committee on the Affairs of the Saratoga and Schenectady Railroad. New York: Sleight and Van Norden, 1833.

The Act of Incorporation of the Rensselaer and Saratoga Railroad Company. New York: Evening Post Steam Press, 1872.

Newspapers and Journals

Albany Gazette. 1829-1833.

American Railroad Journal. 1832-1833.

New York Daily Advertiser. 1829.

Books, Pamphlets, Articles, and Unpublished Works

Abele, Fred B. *The Mohawk and Hudson Railroad Co., 1826-1853.* Schenectady, NY: Mohawk and Hudson Chapter, NRHS, 1981.

Bloodgood, DeWitt S. "Some Account of the Hudson and Mohawk Railroad." *The American Journal of Science and Arts*, XXI, January 1832.

Brown, William H. *The History of the First Locomotives in America.* New York: D. Appleton and Company, 1871.

Carp, Roger E. "The Erie Canal and the Liberal Challenge to Classical Republicanism, 1785-1850." Unpublished PhD Dissertation, 1986, University Microfilms Incorporated.

DeMis, John. "Location of the Original Route of the Mohawk and Hudson Railroad." Unpublished Master's Thesis, New York State Library.

Ellis, David et al. *A History of New York State.* Ithaca, NY: Cornell University Press, 1967.

Faith, Nicholas. *The World Railways Made.* New York: Carroll and Graf, 1991.

FitzSimons, Neal (ed.). *The Reminiscences of John B. Jervis: Engineer of the Old Croton.* Syracuse, NY: Syracuse University Press, 1971.

French, J. H. *Gazetteer of the State of New York.* Syracuse, NY: R.P. Smith, 1860.

Friends of William C. Young. *Biography of William C. Young.* New York: Styles and Cash, 1889.

Harlow, Alvin F. *The Road of the Century: The Story of the New York Central.* New York: Creative Age Press, Inc., 1947.

Hedrick, Ulysses P. *A History of Agriculture in the State of New York.* New York: Hill and Wang, 1966.

Hollingsworth, Brian. *The Illustrated Encyclopedia of the World's Steam Passenger Locomotives.* London: Salamander Books, 1982.

Hungerford, Edward. *Men and Iron: The History of the New York Central.* New York: Thomas Y. Crowell, 1938.

Larkin, F. Daniel. "Erastus Corning," in Robert L. Frey (ed.) *Railroads in the Nineteenth Century, Encyclopedia of American Business History and Biography.* New York: Bruccoli Clark Layman, 1988.

_____. "Erie Railroad," in Robert L. Frey (ed.) *Railroads in the Nineteenth Century, Encyclopedia of*

American Business History and Biography. New York: Bruccoli Clark Layman, 1988.

_____. *John B. Jervis: An American Engineering Pioneer*. Ames, Iowa: Iowa State University Press, 1990.

Munsell, Joel. *Annals of Albany*. Albany, NY: Munsell and Rowland, 1858.

_____. "The Mohawk and Hudson Railroad," *Transactions of the Albany Institute*, 1876, Vol. VIII.

Neu, Irene D. *Erastus Corning: Merchant and Financier, 1794--1872*. Ithaca, N.Y.: Cornell University Press, 1960.

Ola, Per and d'Aulaire, Emily. "Freight Trains are Back and They're On a Roll," *Smithsonian*, June 1995.

Railway and Locomotive Historical Society. *Bulletin #55*. May 1941.

Shaw, Ronald E. *Erie Water West*. Lexington: University of Kentucky Press, 1966.

Spann, Edward K. *The Metropolis: New York City 1840-1857*. New York: Columbia University Press, 1981.

Stevens, Frank W. *The Beginnings of the New York Central Railroad*. New York: G.P. Putnam's Sons, 1926.

Stover, John F. *American Railroads*. Chicago: University of Chicago Press, 1961.

The American Journal of Science and Arts, XXI, January 1832.

Tredgold, Thomas. *A Practical Treatise on Railroads and Carriages*. London: Josiah Taylor, 1825.

Wakefield, Manville B. *Coal Boats to Tidewater*. Fleischmanns, New York: Purple Mountain Press, 1992.

White, John H., Jr. *American Locomotives: An Engineering History, 1830-1880*. Baltimore: Johns Hopkins Press, 1968.

_____. *A History of the American Locomotive: Its Development 1830-1880*. New York: Dover Publications, 1979.

Whitford, Noble E. *History of the Canal System of the State of New York*. Vols. I & II. Albany: Brandon Printing Company, 1906.

Other Sources

Annual Account of Property Passing Eastward and Left at Albany, Utica, and Schenectady Railroad, 1844-45. New York State Library, Albany, NY.

Journal of General Affairs of the Mohawk and Hudson RR Co., 1839-1843. New York State Library, Albany, NY.

Index